# BALANCING ACT

## WEALTH MANAGEMENT
## STRAIGHT TALK FOR WOMEN

### Joslyn G. Ewart

CERTIFIED FINANCIAL PLANNER™ PROFESSIONAL

*Foreword by Jacquelyn Zehner*

*To Linda —*

*Wishing you a lifetime of financial success!*

*Joslyn*

Entrust

FINANCIAL LLC®

**Disclaimer:** *Balancing Act: Wealth Management Straight Talk for Women* is based upon CERTIFIED FINANCIAL PLANNER™ professional Joslyn G. Ewart's experience. It tells the stories of many women as they aim to manage their wealth, protect their style of living, and leave fear behind. With the exception of Danuta Mieloch who graciously granted permission, all names have been changed to protect privacy.

Please remember that past performance may not be indicative of future results. Different types of investments involve varying degrees of risk, and there can be no assurance that the future performance of any specific investment, investment strategy, or product made reference to directly or indirectly in this book will be profitable, meet or exceed any corresponding historical performance, be suitable for your individual situation or prove successful. Due to various factors, including changing market conditions and/or applicable laws, the content in this book may no longer be reflective of current opinions or positions. Entrust Financial LLC® is neither a law firm nor a certified public accounting firm and no portion of this book should be construed as legal or accounting advice.

**Limit of Liability/Disclaimer of Warranty:** While the author has used her best efforts in preparing this book, she makes no representations or warranties with respect to the accuracy or completeness of the contents of this book and specifically disclaims any implied warranties of merchantability or fitness for a particular purpose. The advice and strategies contained herein may not be suitable for your situation. You should consult with a professional where appropriate. Neither the publisher nor authors shall be liable for any loss of profit or any other commercial damages, including but not limited to special, incidental, consequential or other damages.

Aesop's Fables ©2000 by Jerry Pinkney. Used with permission of Chronicle Books, LLC, San Fransisco. Visit ChronicleBooks.com

ISBN: 978-0-9976599-4-8

Printed in the United States of America

**Entrust Financial LLC®**
940 West Valley Road, #1902, Wayne, PA 19087
610-687-3515
www.balancingactbook.com

*Dedicated to my BFF's:*
*Paula, Robyn, and Hannah*

# Acknowledgements

When I reflect on the writing of this book, the image that comes to me is that of a Grand Slam (as baseball fans say). I picture Roy Rasmussen, my book coach who patiently required me to get focused, on third base. Next, I see Dr. Hannah S. Winston, my editor extraordinaire, without whom there would be no book, standing on second base. First base was filled after the manuscript was pretty much finished, when path-finding leader and philanthropist Jacki Zehner agreed to write the Foreword. And finally, the book's home run was hit out of the park by the superb women and men whose stories breathed life into the text. What a team! There could be no better, and for all contributors I am deeply grateful.

## Jacquelyn Zehner

Jacki was the youngest woman and first female trader to become a partner at the global investment bank, Goldman Sachs. She retired from Goldman in 2002, and is now the chief engagement officer and president of Women Moving Millions, a non-profit whose mission is to mobilize unprecedented resources for the advancement of women and girls. It is, at its core, a philanthropic network of over 250 women who have each given a million or more to organizations that focus on girls and women. Collectively, their members have given over a billion dollars.

# Contents

Foreword    ix

Introduction    xiii

## Part I:  Manage Your Wealth    1

Chapter 1: Ascertain Your Current Status    5

Chapter 2: Pinpoint Your Goals    19

Chapter 3: Determine What You Need to Know    37

## Part II:  Protect Your Lifestyle Now
## and into Retirement    55

Chapter 4: Construct a Strong Investment Foundation    57

Chapter 5: Secure Your Financial Independence    77

Chapter 6: Delineate a Retirement Plan    97

## Part III:  Leave Fear Behind    117

Chapter 7: Prepare for the Unexpected    119

Chapter 8: Fulfill Your Charitable Aspirations    135

Chapter 9: Pursue Your Leadership Potential    153

# Foreword

Get ready. I am going to invite you to read a word; then close your eyes and be ready to receive; then recall what comes to mind.

That word is MONEY.

Repeat the word to yourself, now close your eyes, and without judgment receive what comes into your mind. Now take a pen and write those words down, perhaps on this page, on the back cover, on a separate piece of paper. And just let those words be.

We all have money associations, or as Joslyn Ewart calls them, money messages. Some of those messages may serve us well, and others, not so much. This book is about helping you come to terms with your own associations around money and setting you on a path to financial health and empowerment.

So what was my money story?

I grew up in a household where both my parents worked full-time outside the home to provide for our family. I did not grow up with a scarcity mindset, but not an abundance mindset either. Money was what you worked to get, and for me, that was the most influential money message. I started working for money when I was fourteen. My first job was at the concession stand in the local hockey arena (I'm Canadian), then on to a variety of retail roles, all at close to minimum wage.

While in college, I realized that a professional future in financial services was a great way to both have an interesting career and make a lot of money. The chosen path was to get a degree in finance, and I was fortunate to land a job as an analyst at Goldman Sachs in New York City in 1988. My career on Wall Street began, and for the next fourteen years money is what I thought about all day, every day. I was a fixed income bond trader, mortgage-backed bonds to be more specific, and one of the few women in such a role.

I saw that money really did make the world go around, and I also saw that few women were in decision-making roles around money. That ignited my passion to champion women's inclusion and advancement not only as finance professionals, but more generally. Women and money were not two words that people seemed to put together, but my personal narrative told a different story. Add the word *power* to that equation, and that has been the story I have been championing ever since. Women + Money + Power = Possibility.

With a background as a trader and an academic history in the area of finance, you might think I knew a lot about managing my own financial resources, but I did not. While working full-time, with a husband who was doing the same, and two young children to take care of, I did what most people tend to do—and put that kind of decision-making off. Our hard-earned cash stayed in just that, cash, and when Goldman Sachs went public I had a lot more of it. Well, cash and Goldman Sachs stock.

Somewhat counterintuitively, it was when I left Goldman in 2002 that my journey to understand how I might invest my money for positive return really began. I came together with a small group of other amazing women who were in a similar position, and we formed a peer-to-peer learning community where the goal was to leverage our individual and collective efforts to optimize the management of our financial resources. Over the next eight years we met with hundreds of professionals in the financial services sector, while implementing our own investment and philanthropic strategies. I aspired to be an expert so I could not only act on that knowledge personally, but share it with anyone who would listen.

So what is my most important learning from all of this time and effort? Just start somewhere, and then keep going. And by picking up this book, you already are.

Learning by doing is the way to take ownership of your financial life. Money is a tool. It is something we need, and is used to help us live our lives and serve our values. As women especially, we are often given messages around money that do not serve us, and when we realize that, we can get rid of them, ignore them, burn them. Surround yourself with empowering money messages, and seek out the help you need to use this powerful tool to help you lead the life you want to live.

Today, I have a very cool job with a very cool title. My title is chief engagement officer of Women Moving Millions. It is a volunteer job where I spend my time championing for women to use their resources, and especially their financial resources, in support of other women. Increasingly, women are the holders of wealth, and yet studies have shown that women are not as actively involved in managing it as men. Not surprising, and that is why we need books like this one.

In the pages that follow, Joslyn Ewart shares her story of why she became a financial advisor and what she has learned helping other women, like you, become financially empowered. She tells their stories in hopes they will connect with your own and motivate YOU to take charge.

One of my favorite quotes is from Harold Goddard, and it reads: "The destiny of the world is determined less by battles that are lost and won than by the stories it loves and believes in." So I invite you to be part of the collective story of women taking control of their money and using it as the powerful tool that it is—a tool that can serve our families, our values, ourselves.

—Jacquelyn Zehner

# Introduction

Effective wealth management can pose a formidable challenge because it requires making choices based on one's values, needs, and interests. The very nature of choice means selecting between at least two possibilities. This selection process, coupled with the worry that you do not know enough to make the right decisions, can produce surprisingly strong and often conflicted feelings. In fact, the spectrum of your feelings may include frustration, anger, and even paralyzing fear. Not surprisingly, effective wealth management is a complex balancing act.

Strange though it may seem, conflicted feelings sparked by addressing one's personal finances often occur because of our tendency as adults to mimic what we experienced when growing up. We unconsciously replay past financial behaviors and unresolved feelings about money, what I call "money messages." These behaviors and unresolved feelings can become our comfort zone over time, simply because they are so familiar.

When I reflect on the money messages of my childhood, I realize why it took me years to move on from my early lessons. My parents surrounded the subject of money with a good deal of frustration and limitation. The painful emotion of limitation gradually became hardwired as our family's financial norm.

For example, my mother's favorite rant, repeated day in and day out, went something like this: "Dear Heavenly Father, I don't know what I'm going to do. We're already out of money, and your father doesn't get paid for two more weeks! I don't know how we're even going to eat for the rest of the month."

By the time I was six years old, I remember wondering why my parents—who were intelligent and were both college educated (in an era when that was not commonplace)—kept repeating their patterns of frustration and limitation about money. Did money, I wondered, have to be a constant worry? Did money have to be the source of so much fear?

My intention to live differently from what then surrounded me financially was taking shape. I did not want to worry about money. I did not want to live in constant fear of running out of money, or of not having enough money. Looking back, I believe my intention to learn what I needed to know to be able to take care of myself was essentially set before I left elementary school.

This intention to take care of myself started with babysitting, lots of it. I expanded my babysitting roles into housekeeping and cooking chores for the working mothers for whom I worked. They loved the time and effort I saved them and inched up my hourly rate without my even asking. Finally, I was old enough to waitress. Wow! Thanks to tips, I earned about four times the minimum wage, even though I was not yet old enough to serve alcohol.

The next major step of my journey included completing college and landing my first "real" job. I was hired right out of college to be a classroom music teacher for the school district of Philadelphia. I was excited my first day of teaching in September, 1974, because I had achieved a bi-weekly paycheck and a steady job. I had a career! Meanwhile, that same year my favorite grandmother showed me her survivor pension statement.

She received a monthly survivor pension benefit from the pension system to which I now contributed as a teacher in Pennsylvania. This pension system was touted to be excellent and was thought to be a real perk for all teachers. Following the recent death of my grandfather, my grandmother had been awarded a survivor income of $200 per month—or $2,400 per year. In reality, her "excellent" survivor pension, even in 1974, was barely enough to put gas in her car and food on her table.

Although I continued to be excited about earning a paycheck, my grandmother's experience illustrated that I needed to plan for tomorrow, too. I could not just assume, as so many of my new teacher colleagues did, that there would be plenty of money down the road because of our promised pension.

With my steady job and paycheck in place, what did I need to do next to ensure plenty of money down the road? I had a dim awareness that investing in mutual funds could earn me more than the 4 percent fixed interest attributed to my pension contributions. And I knew, from the annuity guy who tried to drum up business in the lunchroom at work, teachers could invest in mutual funds by contributing to a so-called supplemental 403(b) plan.

I recall being rather fearful about sitting down with the annuity guy since I didn't know him and we would be discussing a subject I didn't understand—investing. I was guessing he would probably try to pull a fast one, but knew that at the very least I would be able to see my contributions going into my new account and not his pocket.

Actually, he did pull a fast one, but did so in a way that helped me more than him. Here is what he did: as we discussed the amount of my contributions, he informed me that I had to contribute a minimum of $100 per pay period, or $2,600 per year, to open a supplemental 403(b) plan. I believed him, especially since that didn't seem like much money.

However, to put that small sum into perspective, I was only earning $9,200 *per year* in my third year of teaching. Contributing $2,600 of that small salary into a supplemental retirement plan was sizable for me. I later learned that the minimum contribution allowable was actually $25 per pay period or just $650 per year. The annuity guy was looking to increase his compensation. My benefit was the solid base I built in my retirement portfolio.

My consistent investing year after year ultimately set the stage for me to jump ship from my teaching career in 1996. During my two decades of teaching, the world had gone through a sea change. Women were no longer limited to careers in teaching, nursing, or secretarial work. Unprecedented career opportunities had opened up for women. The world and I were now ready for me to answer my true calling.

My true calling springs from my deepest passion, which is to help others make the right choices at pivotal times in their lives—preferably without financial concerns—just as I have been able to do.

This book will share with you how to manage your wealth, protect your style of living now and into retirement, and leave fear behind. To reiterate, the objective of this book is to help you learn:

- How to ascertain your current status
- How to pinpoint your financial goals
- How to determine what you need to know
- How to construct a strong investment foundation
- How to secure your financial independence
- How to delineate a retirement plan
- How prepare for the unexpected
- How to fulfill your charitable aspirations
- How to pursue your leadership potential

Just as I have been able to do, making the right choices at pivotal times in your life based upon your values, interests, and needs—without financial concerns—offers you the opportunity to move beyond fear and utilize your money with confidence. It begins with the need to understand how to manage your wealth.

# PART I

# Manage Your Wealth

*"It isn't where you came from,
it's where you're going that counts."*

—Ella Fitzgerald

Balancing your values, needs, and interests with respect to your personal finances requires a basic understanding of how to manage your wealth. Most of us, for instance, value knowing we are able to provide well for our family. Our hearts rest easier when we know our loved ones—our spouse, children, and grandchildren—have what they need and want for a comfortable lifestyle. But with today's unprecedented longevity, fulfilling this desire can be fraught with worry. One common concern goes something like this: "If I help my son or my daughter, will I have enough money when I retire? Or will I *outlive* my money?"

Madeleine, a client, faced this type of concern. She scheduled a meeting with me because she wanted to obtain a lump sum distribution from her trust portfolio but was worried about doing so. She began our conversation with a description of the purpose of the trust and her understanding of the restrictive nature of the trust documents. Madeleine reported that her father, a wise man with serious cardiac disease, had devised a wealth management plan in order to enable his wife,

Madeleine's mother, to maintain a comfortable lifestyle after his death. Not only was that goal fulfilled, but now Madeleine was the beneficiary of his financial acumen. Like mom, she too was enjoying a comfortable lifestyle. And one day, mom's sizable trust portfolio would pass to Madeleine's daughter.

Moreover, years ago when dad originally drafted his trust, he stipulated that his lawyers use restrictive language to clarify his intentions to provide a monthly income for his wife and her future recipients. Any request for additional funds would require the agreement of a trustee. The language restrictions were put in place to protect Madeleine's mother and then Madeleine herself from an offspring who wanted an advance or loan from the family trust; in other words, to make it easy to say no. Conversely, the need for trustee agreement also made it difficult for Madeleine to distribute a lump sum when she needed one.

Madeleine's daughter and son-in-law had just become pregnant with their first child. Because their high-powered jobs required frequent out-of-town travel and long working hours, and since Madeleine was now fully retired from her consulting work, they asked her to be on hand to manage child care and nannies when they needed to travel. How thrilling to be instrumental in the care of her first grandchild! Madeleine's heart immediately responded, "Yes." But what should she do? She lived in a different city and she was not interested in giving up her home of forty years.

The logical solution was to purchase a condo near her new grandchild, using a sizable distribution from her trust. But this thought sent questions swirling through her mind: "Can I afford to take a large distribution from my trust? If I do, my monthly trust income will be reduced. Can I afford to live on a lower income—especially with the expense of two homes instead of one? How can I negotiate with my trustee to obtain a one-time major distribution?"

Careful review of Madeleine's wealth plan showed there was no need to worry about outliving her money, even after taking a major lump sum distribution to purchase a second home. Fortunately, we were able to identify a perfect negotiating strategy for the conversation with her trustee. In the end, her trustee was able to bless the lump sum distribution she needed, and Madeleine was able to say yes to her daughter.

Madeleine faced complexity as she aimed to balance the value she placed on helping her family with the need to avoid jeopardizing her own financial well-being. As you can see, preparing to provide well for your family and yourself requires you to consider multiple elements, beginning with your current status.

Your current status—like Madeleine sharing with me the details of her father's wealth planning—is step one. From there it is necessary to pinpoint goals, just as Madeleine identified her goal of distributing a lump sum. The next step is to discover what you need to know prior to taking action. For instance, Madeleine needed a strategy for negotiating with her trustee, and she needed to know what her reduced trust income would be, as well as whether or not her comfortable lifestyle would be diminished by the lower monthly income. Our discussion of how to manage your wealth begins with how to ascertain your current status.

# CHAPTER 1

# Ascertain Your Current Status

The first step in managing your wealth requires you to simply ascertain and embrace where you are now. If you could use your in-car GPS navigation system, it would astutely target your starting place and would draw you a map of the best route to reach your destination. When it comes to your personal finances, however, you will have to develop this roadmap for yourself, beginning with an honest assessment of your current status.

If you are not perfectly clear about the state of your finances at this moment, you are like many of us who are endlessly distracted by the rapid pace of change in our lives. With so little free time at our disposal, it is easy to rationalize that our finances are okay for now and that we have sufficient knowledge of what is going on. Take the case of Janet, who told me, "I know exactly where I am today; I can rattle off all the details to you when we meet."

Janet is a senior-level executive in a technology company who I thought loved numbers and was compulsive enough to have catalogued in her head the precise details of her personal finances. In fact, when she arrived for our first meeting, those details were not at all transparent.

Notably, Janet arrived with an inventory of her account usernames and passwords listed on her smart-phone, making it possible, at least, to find her accounts. But much to my surprise, she also brought along numerous shopping bags full of unopened mail—so many bags in fact, that she needed help getting through the door. As an executive, Janet was a "take charge" kind of person whose work life was filled with distractions, travel, and constant change. When she was able to grab a few minutes to relax, she chose not to spend time cataloging accounts or organizing unopened mail, much of which contained personal financial documents. Generally speaking, it is necessary to assemble and organize financial documents in order to determine your current status. Tips for developing a housekeeping routine will be addressed next.

## Financial Housekeeping

Gathering together your financial and related documents is the perfect starting place for ascertaining your current financial status. To get you started, here is a basic list of items to assemble:

- Tax returns, preferably for the three most recent years
- Income information, such as pay stub(s), 1099s, Social Security statement(s), other
- Information regarding your employee benefits package, including all long-term incentives (LTIs)
- Retirement plan statements, such as employee pension, 401(k), SEP IRA, Keogh, IRA, 403(b), other
- Bank statements for savings/checking accounts, money market funds, CDs
- Brokerage account statements for: stocks, bonds, mutual funds
- Insurance policies/contracts for life, disability, long-term care, annuities
- Financial statements regarding other assets such as: residence, vacation or investment real estate, art, collectibles
- Business statements, such as balance sheets (current and previous few years), profit-and-loss statements, buy-out agreements
- Divorce settlement agreement
- Estate planning and trust documents (re: anticipated inheritance, etc.)

Start collecting documents that are pertinent to your particular situation and organize them in binders, in hanging files, or electronically. Two online resources often used for personal finance storage are: **www.Quicken.com** and **www.mint.com**.

If you have a tendency to procrastinate, give yourself a deadline for organizing the details of your personal finances. For instance, one week is generally enough time for most people. Remember, the details will not take care of themselves. Please note, too, that we all face a retrieval challenge on the internet. Downloads or screenshots usually provide partial information rather than comprehensive statements about your assets. Betsy's story illustrates what I mean.

When a prospective client, Betsy, visited my office for the first time, she provided us with a screenshot of her pre-tax retirement account. At that time her account was valued at just over $2 million. All funds reported on her screenshot were attributed to the same pre-tax registration. This meant that, upon retirement, 100 percent of her account would be fully taxable. But as we talked, I learned she had also contributed some funds over the years on an after-tax basis. Unfortunately, the download Betsy provided did not identify precisely how much of her account had been contributed on an after-tax basis. To avoid being taxed later, when she distributed income in retirement, it was crucial for Betsy to distinguish how much she had contributed pre-tax from how much she had contributed after-tax.

Meanwhile, Betsy assumed that screenshots provided comprehensive information about her investment account. Now, she realized she had to seek additional information. She revisited her company's retirement account website, and was able to locate and print her full quarterly statement. This full statement showed a total of $250,000 in after-tax contributions over the past twenty years.

What a difference that clarification made. I was able to help Betsy see how the after-tax contributions would reduce her income tax bill when she distributed income from the account in retirement. No one wants to miss an opportunity like this.

As you can see, Betsy experienced almost immediate payback when she took the time to gather full statements of her assets rather than just screen shots. Each of us has a somewhat different financial situation. However, until we do our homework, there is no way to know if we, too, might discover financial opportunities.

Doris provides another illustration of the benefits of doing homework. At the beginning of the process, Doris was reluctant to begin gathering together her documents because she was embarrassed about the hit-or-miss quality of her record-keeping. Upon graduation from college in 1967, Doris was employed for eleven years by a public school district in Pennsylvania. It had never occurred to her to save her paycheck information from those early years. Thus, she did not have "proof" of her earnings on which the teacher's pension benefit is based.

We solved that problem by contacting the Social Security administration that had the history of all her reported income. While the task required time and patience, proof of Doris's school district service and earnings was at last unearthed. The result for her was a lifetime pension of $24,000 per year.

I hope by now, like Janet, Betsy, and Doris, you are starting to feel motivated to overcome feelings of inertia or frustration, just knowing how to begin to ascertain your current status. Congratulate yourself for starting your own journey to financial security and independence.

## Release Resistance

Despite feeling enthusiasm about your personal financial journey, it may be difficult to find time to complete the necessary tasks. If you are procrastinating, there could be some unconscious thoughts holding you back. For instance, common points of resistance are frequently associated with childhood money messages and old habits.

Take a moment to consider your answers to this question: "What money messages did I get growing up?" I mentioned earlier that my family taught me that money was synonymous with limitation. Perhaps in your family, money was spent freely, saved religiously, worried about constantly, or a topic that was avoided altogether. It is important to recognize the lessons you were taught, not necessarily to judge the lessons, but simply to identify them. You can determine which lessons continue to serve you well and which ones need to be released. Following is the narrative of a couple that illustrates the need to identify what their families taught them about money.

Jeff and Denise desperately needed to identify the lessons they had been taught about money growing up. Their financial dysfunction as a couple threatened their relationship. When they entered my office the morning of our initial consultation, Jeff appeared friendly but cautious. Denise's face, however, was clouded by a scowl. Early in our conversation I asked each of them to answer this question, "What money messages did you get growing up?" After nearly an hour into our session, Denise began to relax and her scowl began to soften. She tentatively started to enjoy our conversation.

I believe she began to relax when she realized a couple of things. First, her answers did not have to match Jeff's—they could each have different but equally valid perspectives. And second, I was not the only one gaining insight.

Denise was surprised to be learning new things about Jeff, and about their financial interaction as a couple. The revelations were not at all what she had expected. In fact, their respective responses to the money messages question proved to be a turning point for them. For the first time, they realized that each had grown up in a family that routinely lived beyond their means. The financial "norm" they had both experienced as young people was to borrow in order to spend more. Saving first before making major purchases was never an option considered by either Denise's or Jeff's family.

This revelation was both shocking and liberating to both of them. Before our meeting the big question on their minds was, "Why do we always sink deeper into debt and then always have to dig out of debt?" They were smart people, made a lot of money, hated being in debt, and did not want to distribute from retirement plans to pay down debt. Now they understood the origin of their spending patterns.

Perhaps you are fortunate and did not learn damaging money messages as a child. Nevertheless, you still feel reluctant to come to terms with reality. Perhaps, when you talk to your spouse about money, one of you disagrees or gets angry. Maybe you feel your spouse is trying to control you by seeming to always disagree. Or perhaps neither of you feels heard so you are unable to build consensus about financial choices. Conversations about money seem unresolved because of either friction or frustration.

For those who are single, financial tension can be equally compelling. One illustration is when the head screams, "I can't believe you just spent money on that!" not long after a heartfelt spending choice is made. Although a single individual answers only to herself, this type of dueling head and heart internal banter is a recipe for tension. If you want to experience a financial life characterized by confidence rather than tension, you probably need to understand your money personality.

## Money Personalities

"Money personality" is the term often used to designate your subliminal instincts or unconscious perspectives about money. Each of us has one. And our money personality often triggers our most natural responses to any financial choice facing us. For couples, the money personality of one spouse is often the direct opposite of the money personality of the other. No wonder financial clashes destroy more marriages than sexual incompatibilities.

I have found it useful to identify money personalities in the most straightforward manner. Therefore, I have identified the following four types to provide the descriptive framework for the ensuing discussion:

- **Spender:** "I'm almost ready to save. I just need to take care of this one thing…"
- **Saver:** Enjoys the feeling of having money "put away." Already knows what she needs for a secure retirement; is on track.
- **Worrier:** Thinks and talks continuously about money; frequently comments on how much things cost. May obsess about and check her investments online daily.
- **Avoider:** Ignores financial matters, hoping everything will turn out alright.

I suppose as you read through the descriptive list you immediately recognized your own money personality. But in case you are trying to select the "best" one, I am happy to remind you this is not a test. There is no good or bad money personality. Your money personality is simply a characteristic—like hair color. And just as you can change your hair color, you can modify your instinctive reactions and responses to money matters. But you will need to be cognizant of tendencies.

For example, I epitomize the spender money personality. Many people assume that because I am a financial advisor, the only interest I have is saving money. In my case, that is not true. I love spending money. I love the perks money can buy. How delicious it is to think that when I want to go to a specific performance at the Metropolitan Opera in New York City, I can simply pick up the phone and purchase choice seats, without having to worry that because I made a luxurious purchase some other bill won't get paid.

That being said, I also recognize the value of saving. As I reported in the introduction, I started saving for the future in my early twenties because a number of events helped me get started. First and foremost, I was inclined to think about the future. I had no desire to be poor like I was growing up. Finally, it never occurred to me to expect wealthy Prince Charming to miraculously appear and take care of me.

**Spenders** are distinguished by actively thinking about the next thing they want to buy. Their instincts are in direct opposition to the **saver** personality, who is energized by building up her savings and by spending as little as possible. It can be difficult for a spender to set limits and equally difficult for a saver to enjoy her money. Specifically because savers find it difficult to enjoy spending, I have known them to deprive themselves of salon services when they need to cut, dye, and perm their hair. Because they experience these services as expensive, they resort to do-it-yourself measures. The most extreme savers I have encountered were a Massachusetts couple who kept the heat in their home at 55° all winter long. Paying for fuel to stay warm was too expensive in their view. Yet, this couple's net worth exceeded $12 million.

Now, let us examine the characteristics of the **worrier**. As you may recall in the Introduction, I described my mother as a worrier. It may come as a surprise to learn worriers do not routinely make informed decisions about their money, despite all that worrying; nor do they necessarily save to alleviate their worry. They simply worry all the time. Money is always on their minds. Just for fun, when I was eight years old, I spent an hour counting the number of times my mother mentioned money—e.g., not having enough money, being out of money, thinking *everything* cost more than she could afford, and so forth. I discovered during that hour she mentioned money at least once every minute. How I wished I could stop all her worrying. Of course, only she could make that happen.

Finally, money **avoiders** are people who would be happy if money just disappeared from the earth. They are not interested in thinking about money, talking about it, or planning for it. For example, they often tip their hand to their financial advisor in the following manner: money avoiders schedule a meeting, reschedule a few days later when something comes up, reschedule a second time when another conflict surfaces. Finally, on the third try they reschedule their appointment and manage to keep the date.

Do not be surprised to discover characteristics of more than one money personality in yourself. But whether you discover them or not, before making financial decisions—especially major ones—identify the instincts motivating your course of action. This extra degree of thoughtfulness in all likelihood will enable you to make informed decisions.

## What Is Personally Important about Money?

Thus far you have learned the importance of assessing where you are financially and some common points of resistance. With all the tasks you have to accomplish in your daily life, it may seem easier to put aside thoughts of your personal finances and avoid dealing with them until you have to—for instance, when you are on the cusp of retirement.

While determining a timetable for getting serious about your financial well-being is a matter of personal choice, in my experience, the sooner you get your money working for you (rather than you simply working for it), the more choices you will ultimately have. The more choices you have, the more control you will feel in your everyday life. And the more control you experience, the more opportunities you will have to fulfill your values. That brings us to the question: what are your personal finance values?

The work of Bill Bachrach has been instrumental in helping thousands of individuals identify their most important values regarding money. An Iron Man competitor, Bill coined this question: "What's important about money, to you?" This question is his opener for what he calls "the values conversation."

You can pursue the values conversation by yourself, with your spouse, or with someone you trust. Begin by having a conversation with yourself, in which you ask yourself, "What's important about money, to me?" Jot down your answers in a stream-of-consciousness fashion, trying not to evaluate your answers. The point here is to get as close as possible to what matters most to you. And remember, your spouse or loved one is not likely to have the same responses because we all express ourselves differently.

Answers I have heard frequently from clients include:

- Taking care of my family
- Not running out
- Being able to do what I want
- Having financial independence
- Keeping the lifestyle I have
- Having financial security
- Feeling comfortable

A favorite example of the differences in values spouses express unfolded in my office several years ago. It involved a lovely couple, Jerry and Laura, who had been married for decades, lived within their means, and had been very careful with their money. They were faced with deciding what to do with some extra income they had acquired.

Laura was the family budgeter and bill-payer and was thrilled that extra income had flowed into their checking account. But she didn't need the funds for current expenses. They were doing just fine with the income they had. So Laura wanted to give the extra money to their recently married daughter and new son-in-law. How fabulous it would be to provide them with the down payment for their first home.

"Whoa!" Jerry said, "No way. We already gave her a college education and helped her with graduate school expenses. That money is mine, and I'm buying a Corvette. I'm seventy years old. This is my last chance." In the seconds after Jerry uttered that remark, Laura looked ready to murder him in my comfortable conference room. "You don't need a Corvette," she retorted. "It will just sit in the garage like a sculpture. And nobody will even see it. That money is going to our daughter!"

Being a car lover myself, I asked Jerry, "What color?" I then proceeded to discover how much money he needed to purchase his car and how much money Laura needed to give to their daughter. Once all their values were revealed, we were able to construct a plan that gave both Jerry and Laura what they wanted.

As Jerry and Laura's case indicates, values yield different financial priorities. Nine times out of ten all needs can be met, but you have to know what is important to each player. Identifying their values is often the lynchpin.

Another challenge that may surface for some couples is values that conflict or work at cross purposes. For example, you may be familiar with the expression *hemorrhaging money*. This was the descriptive phrase Emily and Dan used to depict their experience of the steady depletion of money from their household.

In fact, when Emily and Dan contacted my office for an initial meeting, they explained they were calling because they were hemorrhaging money. As it turned out, they were in this predicament because they had not faced the challenge of conflicting values: their zeal to take care of their family regardless of cost was dissipating the funds they needed for their own financial independence.

A review of their portfolio statements showed a dissipation of $2 million dollars over a short period of time. They were both scared. They thought they had been making good decisions, but now were confronted by the reality of running out of money and becoming a burden to their four children.

What had happened? For starters, they had promised to fully fund college educations for each of their four children, regardless of where that child attended school. This promise had extended to full funding of law school for their oldest son, who upon graduation would soon earn an income that exceeded Emily's and Dan's combined income. Then there was the cost of regular therapy for two of their four children, none of which was covered by health insurance. Additionally, there was their promise to pay long-term health care expenses for Emily's mother, who at this stage of life received a small survivor pension and a minimal Social Security benefit. Her need for full nursing care demanded funding at a level well beyond her means. In fact, as Emily and Dan discovered, the cost of mom's care made the annual cost of higher education for their children look almost reasonable.

Within the past couple of years Dan had received a sizable inheritance from his father. The receipt of that inheritance assured them they now had the amount of money they needed to fulfill all the promises they had made. Unfortunately, they had not sat down to run the numbers with precision. And by the time they received the generous inheritance, they already had a lot of old debt accruing high interest rates. Emily and Dan were frustrated and did not know where to begin, to stop hemorrhaging money. I introduced them to strategies they implemented for preventing further asset dissipation.

The steps included:

- Pinpointing their three top extraordinary expenses
- Brainstorming options for meeting these expenses, other than dissipating their portfolio
- Selecting the cash flow options with which they were comfortable

- Creating a timeline for implementing their updated cash flow plan
- Discussing how to have conversations with their four children and Emily's mother about their revised family cash flow plan

A cash flow option they selected involved sharing the repayment of college debt—dollar for dollar—with the child who incurred it. For instance, their younger son had loans of $120,000. Emily and Dan discussed the need for him to pay one dollar for every dollar they paid until the debt was discharged.

Another cash flow strategy they selected regarded reducing the monthly cost of therapy for two children. Emily investigated options and discovered a therapist in their health insurance network whose fees were covered by their plan. With guidance and by implementing changes in how they managed their finances, they stopped hemorrhaging money and resolved their desire to take care of their family without running out of money.

## Balancing Act Implications

Our discussion was launched with the thesis that managing your wealth requires you to ascertain and embrace where you are right now. As we learned, that understanding—supported by an inventory of your financial documents—involves the need to identify your financial values and money messages from the past, as well as to recognize the influences of your money personality.

This can prove challenging because conflicting needs, values, and interests may be uncovered. Addressing them can require a good deal of finesse—particularly when the task is intended to lead to balanced decision-making with respect to your money. Remember Jerry and Laura and the "he wants/she wants" dilemma regarding the use of extra money? It is no wonder most investors choose to work with an independent, objective advisor. One role of an objective advisor is as listener; a good advisor will listen to clients' fears (needs), tease out the issues driving those feelings (values), and provide practical long-term answers (to support their interests).

Help yourself ascertain and embrace where you are right now by completing these two exercises:

### *Exercise #1: Gather Your Documents*

Gather your financial and related documents. This list, also presented earlier in this chapter, is a starting place to help you identify the multiple aspects of your personal finances. Organize the documents in each category in a binder, in hanging files, or electronically. **www.Quicken.com** and **www.mint.com** are two online resources often used for personal finance storage. Good luck!

- Tax returns—preferably for the three most recent years
- Income information, such as pay stub(s), 1099's, Social Security statement(s), other
- Information regarding your employee benefits package, including all long-term incentives (LTI's)
- Retirement plan statements, such as employee pension, 401(k), SEP IRA, Keogh, IRA, 403(b), other
- Bank statements for savings/checking accounts, money market funds, CDs
- Brokerage account statements for stocks, bonds, mutual funds
- Insurance policies/contracts for life, disability, long-term care, annuities
- Financial statements regarding other assets, such as residence, vacation or investment real estate, art, collectibles
- Business statements, such as balance sheets (current and previous few years), profit-and-loss statements, buy-out agreements
- Divorce settlement agreement
- Estate planning and trust documents; expected inheritance

### *Exercise #2: Your Money Personality*

Are you a big spender, saver, worrier, or avoider? Are your decisions driven by more than one money personality perspective? Take a few moments to complete *Your Money Personality Quiz*. Visit **Balancingactbook.com** and click on **Resources,** then **Your Money Personality Quiz**. Besides being fun, this quiz and the scoring of your results will help you better understand your own instinctive responses to financial decisions that confront you.

As Ella Fitzgerald reminded us at the beginning of this chapter, "It is not where we came from, it is where we are going that counts." Take heart from women like Madeleine, Janet, Betsy, Doris, Denise, Laura, and Emily. You, too, now have the tools you need to begin the journey of managing your wealth. And you have set the stage to pinpoint your goals, a task we explore in Chapter 2.

CHAPTER 2

# Pinpoint Your Goals

*"You can do anything you want to do, if you know what to do."*

—Betty Carter

It does not seem to matter to Americans whether or not they were among the first generation to hear Frank Sinatra sing "I'll do it my way." The "my way" philosophy has worked itself into our DNA. But when it comes to managing your wealth, even doing it your way takes effort and calls on you to balance your values, needs, and interests.

Janet, whom we met in Chapter 1, certainly learned it takes effort. She began by assuming her phone list of usernames and passwords for all her financial accounts, in tandem with her bags of unopened mail, meant she was doing it her way. But she quickly learned she was unable to describe the state of her finances. Without putting effort into understanding where she was right now, Janet had no basis for pinpointing her goals for the future. She was simply not prepared to map out her financial journey.

Nor were Jeff and Denise prepared to deal with their personal finances. As you may recall from Chapter 1, they were unable to achieve balance regarding their decision-making because their behaviors continued to unconsciously mimic the money messages they learned in childhood.

It may surprise you to learn how few women, just like Janet and Denise, are actually prepared to plan for or make decisions about their financial future. This may be because in the past women were not expected to have a voice regarding the process of pinpointing their financial goals and this former way of thinking dominates today—despite the phenomenal levels of professional and financial success many women have now achieved.

As we begin the process of identifying your financial goals, the following synthesis of a number of findings reported in *Cultivating the Middle-Class Millionaire*[1] and "Harnessing the Power of the Purse"[2] sheds light on the perspective of many women regarding pinpointing personal finance goals.

Affluent women who have achieved the threshold for high-net-worth status (minimum invested assets of $1 million dollars with average invested assets of $3.5 million dollars) want to do the right thing with their money because money permits them to take care of their family's needs without having to worry and serves as their gateway to personal freedom.

Their interest in and commitment to doing the right thing with their money, however, does not mean the majority are proactive regarding their personal finances. In fact, goal-setting for long-term financial success is often vague and lacks focus. This tendency is partially explained because many women report little interest in the process of investing or wealth management. They describe themselves as fairly conservative in their personal and professional lives and report they simply think of investing as a necessary means to an end.

On the other hand, even women who do describe themselves as

---

[1]Geracioti, David A., and Russ Alan Prince. *Cultivating the Middle-Class Millionaire: Why Financial Advisors Are Failing Their Wealthy Clients and What They Can Do About It.* Johannesburg, South Africa: Primedia, 2005.

[2]Hewlett, Sylvia Ann, Andrea Turner Moffitt, and Melinda Marshall. "Harnessing the Power of the Purse: Female Investors and Global Opportunities for Growth." Center for Talent Innovation.

financially literate still may not put this knowledge to work for their financial well-being because they admit their financial confidence lags notably behind their literacy.

As jazz singer Betty Carter observed, "You can do anything you want to do, if you know what to do." This chapter will help you know what to do—as you aim to identify your financial goals. Three easy steps will form the framework for designing your personal roadmap:

1. Pinpoint

2. Prioritize

3. Proceed

**Pinpoint**, **prioritize**, and **proceed.** What a powerful triple-play of action verbs! We are about to discover how they may be instrumental in establishing and/or enhancing your effectiveness in managing your wealth.

## Three Easy Steps

I am confident that every day of your life you take care to **pinpoint** the look you want when you decide what to wear. Whether you begin the day dressed for professional success or for tennis, your outfit communicates your confidence in knowing exactly what to do for the occasion at hand. You may **prioritize** when to wear a more formal look or a less formal one, depending on whom you will be meeting or what event is scheduled that day. You then **proceed** to implement the look.

**Pinpoint**, **prioritize**, and **proceed.** I imagine you are comfortable with each of these powerful action verbs. In fact, they have probably been instrumental to your success in life. I now encourage you to adopt these three actions as checkpoints on your journey as you prepare to achieve your financial goals.

Step one requires you to **pinpoint** exactly what your goals are. That task completed, step two requires you to **prioritize** your goals; in other words, identify what things need to be addressed first, second, and so forth. Finally you will be ready for step three—**proceed** to implement.

## Step One: Pinpoint

Pinpointing your goals probably sounds easy. After all, you do not need to study up on the stock market to decide what your personal financial goals are. But then again, it is easy to get trapped here in step one because emotionally most of us want as much money as possible. Trying to achieve as much money as possible is not actually a pinpointed goal because it is not precise.

The media unexpectedly provided some useful guidance regarding step one by popularizing the question, "What is my number?" Your number is a precise figure representing the amount of money required to support your style of living in retirement.

The need to know her number prompted Frances, a high-level corporate attorney, to contact our office. Frances is a really smart lady, accustomed to working hard and having the income to show for it. Her first investing experiences were real winners, because they occurred in the late 1990s when "all boats were rising," to borrow a Warren Buffett metaphor.

But then in the early 2000s all boats subsequently began to drop. And Frances's portfolio results went from an annual "Wow!" to declines, and then more declines. You may remember that a three-year declining stock market painfully launched our twenty-first century.

Frances regarded herself as being smart and on top of things, so those declines felt like a hard smack to her. Ready or not she learned in a hurry that none of us controls the capital markets. What we can control is our understanding of how they work and how we choose to implement our portfolios as we aim to benefit from them.

Upon arriving at my office for her discovery meeting, Frances greeted me. Then without pausing or taking a breath, she immediately stated, "I am here because I need to know what my number is."

Let us assume for a moment that just like Frances, you need to know what your number is. As we learned in Chapter 1, the process begins with taking a detailed inventory of what financial resources you currently have. It continues with an understanding of how you (and your spouse, if appropriate) make decisions, remembering to be sensitive to your money personality. Then you need to give voice to your values—that is, articulate what is important for you to achieve with your money.

Clearly, take-charge Frances was hoping for a quick numeric solution to her long-term financial success. But just as the simplest outfit may require multiple decisions to achieve the desired outcome—snug or loose, casual or formal, well-coordinated or off-handed, flat shoes or heels, accessories or no accessories—your answer to "What is my number?" may require you to make multiple decisions.

Although the decisions involved in planning outfits are easy and become second nature over time, creating a plan for maximizing the value of your money is a risky enterprise. Poor financial decisions can lead to expensive mistakes we would rather avoid. After all, if you select the wrong blouse from time to time, who really cares? But if you select the wrong asset allocation for your portfolio, subsequent declines could be devastating.

With Chapter 1 considerations under your belt, it is time to expand your thinking as you aim to make the right choices. The following list offers guidance regarding factors that will likely impact your number. Taking the time to precisely identify each of these factors with respect to your own situation can be essential as you pinpoint your financial goals.

- Your current age
- The age by which you want to have achieved your number
- Dependents for whom you may be/become responsible
- Costs for funding your style of living
- Your current assets and liabilities, and how they are positioned
- Your anticipated longevity
- Your comfort level with capital market risks
- The anticipated inflation rate in the decades ahead

I suspect you now see that making decisions about your money with a sense of confidence is about more than simply adding up numbers or

making a few mathematical calculations. This is because money decisions are first and foremost about what is important to you. They are
about who you are and what impact you want to make.

Like Frances, who sought my help to identify her number after experiencing steep market downturns in her retirement portfolio, Erin was
confronted by circumstances that prompted her to take a closer look at
identifying where she wanted to be. Erin, a married thirty-nine-year-
old working mom with a large number of stock options granted by her
former employer, needed to make a decision about the exercise of her
substantially appreciated options soon, before they expired. Here is an
example of a conversation we had.

"I would like to talk to you sometime," Erin began. "I have some
stock options I need to exercise. Otherwise I will lose them, and I think
they are worth quite a bit. Of course, I hate to think about the taxes I
will owe, so I have procrastinated about doing anything."

In order to grasp more fully what was on her mind I asked, "Are
there other financial issues you are considering, especially since you
mentioned your stock options proceeds may be substantial? Will your
husband be joining us when we meet?"

Erin answered that, in addition to her stock options and tax questions, there were other things on her mind. For one, she had been forced
to change jobs recently. The need to seek a new position had come as a
bolt out of the blue. She had always assumed she would stay with her
previous company until retirement—a situation that pleased her. But
internal changes occurring in the company forced her to seek a new
position elsewhere. Salary level was now a primary concern for Erin
because the salary for her new position was less than she had been earning in her previous job. As the primary wage earner, the new lower
monthly income was beginning to cause worry. Erin assumed they
would still be okay but did not actually have a plan depicting what
"okay" looked like.

According to Erin, her husband had a laissez-faire attitude about
their finances because they had been married for more than two
decades and had always had the income to do whatever they wanted;
to him, that translated into "no need to plan." Because of his attitudes

towards their finances, she didn't know whether he would join us for our meeting.

In addition, Erin worried about her portfolio. Although she thought she owned good stocks, she said that she might need some help with diversification and with making adjustments over time. Again, she admitted she did not have a plan, so as the years passed monitoring her portfolio had always been an afterthought.

Erin was startled into an awareness of her lack of planning by a forced job change, a diminished income as the family's primary wage-earner, and substantially appreciated stock options causing substantial income-tax consequences. Her distress was magnified because she and her husband had not taken the time to pinpoint their financial goals, they did not have a plan for maintaining their current financial success, nor had they identified a number for their future financial security.

Just as the list presented earlier in this chapter helped Frances pinpoint her number, so did the list help Erin focus her thinking. As our planning work proceeded, Erin realized she needed help prioritizing the goals she had pinpointed.

## Step Two: Prioritize

Depending on your own situation, prioritizing your financial goals can be straightforward or complex. If you see your situation as straightforward like Frances did (her number was her goal) you may be ready to prioritize the steps you need to take to achieve your number for retirement.

However, if your situation is complicated like Erin's, you may need to prioritize your goals in terms of importance or timing—short-term versus long-term—*before* identifying the steps you need to take to achieve your goals. For instance, Erin realized that she had two short-term goals and one long-term goal.

Erin's short-term goals:

1. Decide when to exercise her appreciated stock options to get the highest profit. (Tax minimization opportunities influenced her timing.)

2. Optimize her current income. (Identifying strategies to reduce her annual income tax liability was paramount in addressing this concern.)

Erin's long-term goal:

1. Decide what asset allocation decision was likely to help fulfill her long-term investment goals with the least amount of risk. (Identifying the factors—see the list presented earlier in this chapter—that were relevant for pinpointing her number was crucial to this decision.)

Prioritizing her goals helped Erin feel less overwhelmed by her current situation. It allowed her to focus on attaining one goal before moving on to the next one. She reported to me that after she attained her first goal she felt more confident in tackling the second. Particularly because the second goal was thrust on her due to her forced job change and subsequent reduced income, approaching her second short-term goal from a perspective of confidence was empowering.

After addressing these two goals, Erin was ready to focus on her long-term goal regarding her asset allocation decision. It is not uncommon for a number of steps to be involved in pinpointing and then prioritizing goals, just as Erin experienced. For instance, she needed several conversations to fully articulate the complexities of her current situation before she was ready to prioritize her short-term and long-term goals. Frances, on the other hand, was able to clearly articulate her need to know her number within minutes of our greeting one another. Similar to Frances, my clients Suzy and Richard were able to articulate their goals in a straightforward manner during our initial conversation.

When we met for the first time, Suzy and Richard presented their goals to me in what they called their order of importance. "But," they added, "actually they are all equally important because we want to achieve them all." The four goals on their list were:

1. Retire in fifteen years
2. Avoid diminishment of their current style of living when they retired

3. Travel whenever they liked and live abroad from time to time in retirement

4. Leave a charitable legacy, assuming family members did not need financial assistance in the future

While they had pinpointed what they hoped to achieve fifteen years hence, the steps they needed to take—and how to prioritize these steps—remained a mystery to Suzy and Richard. Our discussion regarding these steps unfolded over a series of meetings.

They were gradually able to agree upon the steps that would help them achieve their retirement goals. The three short-term steps they identified were:

- Fully fund their respective retirement savings plans, in the interest of building their retirement nest egg

- Take advantage of Richard's employer's option to pre-fund their lifetime health insurance benefits

- Fund a savings account for unexpected large bills and emergencies (no more reliance on home equity loans with interest payments!)

Suzy and Richard viewed these first three steps as fundamental to achieving their first two goals: retire in fifteen years and avoid diminishment of their current style of living when retired. With these decisions made, they felt ready to address longer-term steps they planned to initiate after the initial steps were well underway. Their longer-term steps were:

- Accelerate their mortgage payments and eliminate that monthly bill within ten years

- Build a retirement travel account, aiming for full funding within twelve years

- As part of their estate planning, consider how much to earmark as inheritance for their two children and how much to earmark as a charitable legacy

The foregoing stories illustrate how very different client goals and priorities can be, and they are but representative examples. Before considering another source of impact on your intentions to plan effectively—the impact of complex family relationships—this short list enumerates several additional longer-term priorities shared by many families with whom I work:

- Preparing to fully fund children's college educations
- Preparing to purchase a vacation home
- Establishing a vacation fund for intergenerational family vacations; many grandparents love taking the whole family away on an annual vacation

The need to prioritize your goals after you precisely pinpoint them—to determine what goal should be addressed first, second, third—sounds self-evident. However, setting priorities can become distressing and complicated, particularly when your carefully honed priorities do not coincide with what your family expects. The following vignette illustrates how the best of intentions can lead to a complex situation.

Lucy is a highly successful executive who has worked diligently for many years in a large corporation, taking advantage of countless opportunities to advance her skills and move up the corporate ladder. She is also the mother of two adult children in their twenties and is a recent widow.

Not long after her husband died, her children began asking her for money. They would say: "Mom, I need a little help right now because I'm running short." She noted it was uncharacteristic of her children to ask their dad for financial support when he was alive, but she loved her son and daughter and wanted to help. After all, the amounts they requested were affordable.

But as time passed she noticed a pattern emerging; apparently her children assumed Lucy had inherited a large sum of money after their father died. And Lucy soon began to fear that by going along with their requests she was sending a number of wrong messages:

1. You can live beyond your means
2. Mom's a gravy train
3. You don't have to work hard to support yourself

Difficult though it was, she decided she had to say no. She realized that by acquiescing to her children's request for "a little help," she was crippling competent adults and preventing them from learning to take responsibility for helping themselves.

## Family Complexities

Other family complexities may also arise that make prioritizing goals a challenge. Aiming to do the right thing with your money may present emotional difficulties for you just as it did for Lucy, and your efforts to abide by your priorities may encounter roadblocks, too.

Continuing with the theme of family complexity, two more examples are becoming increasingly commonplace. The first is the potentially tricky set of relationships one faces as part of a blended family. The second is the potential complexity one faces when an extended family includes a non-traditional relationship.

To begin with, let us discuss the term "blended family." Allegedly, the concept first came into use in the mid-1970s and was used to describe a family made of two parents and their children from previous marriages. A traditional example of a blended family is a woman with a child or children from a previous marriage who marries a man with a child or children from a previous marriage. Simply speaking, a blended family is synonymous with the term step-family. The adults in a step-family may or may not have children together. If they do reproduce, their progeny will exist alongside the step-siblings brought into the family by their respective parent.

Now, suppose your intergenerational family includes a non-traditional component such as a single parent; a co-habiting couple; or a gay, lesbian, bisexual or transgender person. In the case of gay and lesbian couples, increasing numbers are marrying and choosing to become parents. In non-traditional gay or lesbian families there may be two moms or two dads, an egg or sperm donor, or a surrogate. Should either of the spouses have children from a previous marriage, their current non-traditional family would also be considered a blended family.

Although we rarely get to choose the family to which we belong, we do get to decide how to respond to familial exceptions that come our way. Having well-established priorities in place before a crisis occurs can make a huge difference, as Eva learned firsthand. Highlights of her story illustrate a family crisis and the power of pinpointing and prioritizing goals beforehand.

Eva was a member of a blended family for almost thirty years, until the untimely death of her husband, Ralph. Throughout that time Eva's presence in the lives of her husband's four children from a previous marriage was not welcomed but was tolerated with some degree of grace.

Meanwhile, as the years passed, Eva put time and effort into establishing her financial priorities which included creating an emergency funds account, having investments set aside for retirement, paying off her mortgage, and accumulating a considerable sum of discretionary money for enjoying life and giving generously to members of her family. With regard to supporting her family, Eva had established a history of helping her mother financially. Like so many women her age, Eva's mother had not planned for the costs associated with longevity, and she was now in good health approaching the age of 90.

Following her husband's death, Eva decided to help her youngest stepson purchase a home. She and Ralph had always tried to offer this son extra consideration because he was an "odd duck," as the British would say, and no psychological service had been able to shed light on his unique special needs. Several years passed without incident. Then, Eva called me one night to say there was a crisis. Her stepson had been incarcerated, was in big trouble, and needed help. She noted that criminal legal fees are expensive, but without a competent attorney, the charges against her stepson could escalate. Fearing he might ultimately be required to serve more than a decade behind bars, Eva was in a quandary. On the one hand, she wanted to help pay his legal fees. But this would require her to use a substantial amount of her emergency funds, something she had never needed to do in the past. As we talked, Eva expressed hope that by offering to pay some of the legal fees, other contributors would surface to help defray the cost of a lawyer.

Conversely, she feared that when she set limits and refused to pay other fees associated with her stepson's incarceration, intense expressions of anger would likely surface. And what if her offer to pay for a lawyer led his siblings to make their own requests for money?

What Eva could never have predicted was the emotional curveball that was coming her way. When she made the offer to help pay the cost of her stepson's legal fees, she soon found herself shunned by her other stepchildren. Apparently they perceived her offer to help as meddling in family business. She suddenly realized she was not considered a member of the family. Nevertheless, Eva chose to hold fast to her convictions. Because her priority was to help reduce her stepson's jail time, she agreed to pay the attorney's fees. But, she would not honor other financial requests. Upon his release from jail some years later, her stepson would have to cobble together available public resources to satisfy his creditors. He would simply have to rely on public agencies intended to help people in circumstances like his.

When the case finally resolved, I received another call from Eva. "Whew!" she said, "The good news is that hiring a competent attorney greatly reduced the charges against my stepson, and therefore the length of his prison term. The bad news is that while I certainly predicted expressions of anger, I could never have predicted the severing of family ties I had carefully nurtured for thirty years."

She continued, "I surely am glad my financial priorities were in order before this crisis hit. Otherwise, as family tensions escalated, I am not sure how I would have managed. Without that financial structure in place, I think I would have felt in the middle of an emotional and financial slaughter—my own."

Before segueing to a discussion of **Step Three: Proceed**, let us take a moment to review what has been discussed thus far. The first step in identifying your goals is to pinpoint your aims. At the most basic level this aim often involves establishing your number—the amount of money you need to set aside in order to maintain your style of living.

After pinpointing your objectives you need to prioritize them. Just like Erin, you may discover you need to prioritize short-term aims followed by your long-term aims. Suzy and Richard were good at pinpointing their future aspirations in order of importance, but needed

assistance formulating the steps to take and specifying timelines for fulfilling their retirement priorities.

We are about to meet Arielle and James. Like Eva, they had already
pinpointed their aims and prioritized them. But when unexpected
events occurred, they were forced to re-evaluate their carefully formulated plan.

## Step Three: Proceed

Arielle and her husband James were proud of the progress they had
made with respect to their retirement planning. The primary goal of
their financial game plan was straightforward: each of them would stop
working full-time in eight years.

Arielle had carefully identified their financial goals and then num-
bered them in order of importance. In her mind their plan was set.
According to the plan, they would tackle one major funding goal each
year for the next six years, and at the end of each year she and James
would assess their success in meeting the year's goal. With six goals
and eight years until retirement, they were allowing themselves two
extra years to fund any goals not satisfied.

Arielle was visual and liked to see their financial game plan at a
glance. To that end, I helped them design a timeline, *Proceed to Retirement* (Figure 1), to serve as a graphic image of their progress.

We had barely finished creating her *Proceed to Retirement* timeline
when they received devastating news. James was diagnosed with a
chronic and potentially debilitating disease and Arielle was in a state of
shock. There had been no warning and James was not yet sixty years
old. He had always been so healthy. As thoughts swirled through her
mind, Arielle began to wonder: "Do I need to re-think my retirement
goal? Are my priorities still in the right order? Should I proceed to
implement even though James is ill? What am I forgetting to think
about?"

Whenever she felt anxiety rise, she calmed herself down, knowing
it would not help James to see her panic-stricken. Arielle needed to feel
financially secure and knew it was important to protect their style of

# Proceed to Retirement
### Arielle and James
### Primary goal: Retire in eight years

## Priorities and Funding Resources

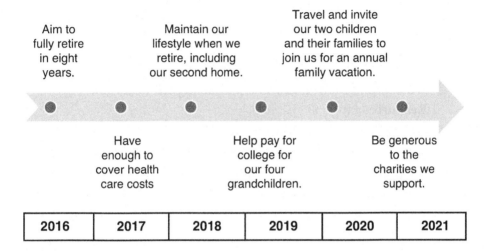

Aim to fully retire in eight years.

Maintain our lifestyle when we retire, including our second home.

Travel and invite our two children and their families to join us for an annual family vacation.

Have enough to cover health care costs

Help pay for college for our four grandchildren.

Be generous to the charities we support.

| 2016 | 2017 | 2018 | 2019 | 2020 | 2021 |

## Year Fulfilled

### Income/distributions

Social security benefits
Investment dividends and interest
IRA required minimum portfolio distributions
Discretionary, Inherited account

### Portfolio acount

Cash
JTWROS account
IRA, James; IRA, Arielle
Inheritance, Arielle

**Figure 1:** Proceed to Retirement

living. In spite of everything, she and James never wanted to become a burden to their children. Of course they would seek the best available medical treatment for James. In the meantime, addressing their personal finances would give her focus. Now there was even more reason to proceed without delay. Arielle identified an additional priority. Now, she recognized the need for more flexibility in their financial plan because they might need to abruptly shift gears on a dime and revise their priorities if the future demanded it. So she and James resolved to double the amount of available cash to tap into for an emergency.

As you make plans to proceed, I encourage you to start by selecting a graphic organizer that suits you. The following is a list of tools you might find useful as you begin making a visual of your personal finances:

1. A *Four Quadrants Chart* (**balancingactbook.com**, **Resources** tab)

2. A *Financial Priorities Timeline* (**balancingactbook.com**, **Resources** tab)

3. Online resources you already use to maintain your financial accounts. Expand your use beyond, "Am I on track to achieve my portfolio goals by my retirement date?" Include your prioritized goals. Add in dates indicating when you intend to achieve each goal. Make notes of other considerations that may impact your success.

Regardless of which diagram you use, remember to list all your financial resources. Keeping a current list of your resources helps you connect the dots between each goal and the source of funding for that goal. Should any of your funding resources change, it may signal the need to revise your goals, too.

Our virtual world notwithstanding, I suggest you confine your visual to one piece of paper because you will find it powerful to be able to represent your financial game plan succinctly on a single sheet of paper. Simplicity leads more easily to clarity of vision, and a clear vision is likely to result in the achievement of your goals.

## Balancing Act Implications

By now you probably sense that pinpointing goals is a complex task. Being precise, prioritizing, and adopting a flexible stance when proceeding, particularly when circumstances change, is not easy. Organizing all the details can feel like running an obstacle course and is accompanied by high-stakes chances for missteps. Remember how Arielle had to revisit her carefully laid plans in the face of James' unexpected medical needs? Not surprisingly, the complexity of goal identification is magnified because the task is addressed within the context of balancing your values, needs, and interests.

To help navigate these multi-faceted concerns successfully, most affluent women partner with an "expert" advisor. The advisor aims to provide client-centered expertise in assessing the state of clients' finances and to develop risk-aware strategies, thus avoiding what could have been high-stakes missteps. As you have probably ascertained, my team and I love to partner with clients as they aim to address their complex concerns within the context of their whole style of living. I encourage you to contact us at 610-687-3515 or **info@entrustfinancial.com** to start a conversation about your personal finances.

As you consider reaching out, it is important to remember that even in situations where there seem to be no obstacles, financial success rarely hinges on how competent a woman is. I am reminded of a cool-headed elementary school teacher who demonstrated sound judgment in the classroom in the face of difficult management conditions, but at home claimed to display nothing but highly emotional responses when dealing with her own children. As she used to report, "My sons get away with murder. I can't discipline *them* at all." Likewise, a successful woman might be cool-headed about financial matters when at work and decidedly less than cool-headed handling financial decisions at home.

The following two exercises will help you start identifying your financial goals.

### *Exercise #1: Factors that Impact Your Number*

This activity is designed to help you gather the preliminary data you need to follow the three easy steps (pinpoint, prioritize, proceed) presented in this chapter.

Earlier in the chapter a list of factors was provided that will likely impact your number. Specifically, these factors are intended to guide your thinking as you aim to pinpoint your financial goals, remembering that trying to accumulate "as much money as possible" is not a precise goal. The factors are:

- Your current age
- The age by which you want to have achieved your number
- Dependents for whom you may be/become responsible
- Costs for funding your style of living
- Your current assets and liabilities, and how they are positioned
- Your anticipated longevity
- Your comfort level with capital market risks
- The anticipated inflation rate in the decades ahead

With this information in hand, you will be ready for Exercise #2.

### Exercise #2: Graphic Organizers

Visit **Balancingactbook.com** and click on the **Resources** tab. Select your preferred graphic organizer from Chapter 2, *Four Quadrants Chart*, or Chapter 2, *Financial Priorities Timeline*, in order to pinpoint your goals. Then, prioritize them, specify your timelines for completion, and inventory the financial resources you have available to fund your aspirations. Remember to keep your inventory of financial resources current with respect to your income sources and investments, especially if there are material changes in your financial situation.

Make every effort to confine your visual to one piece of paper. Feel the power of this succinct representation of your plan. Now you are ready to proceed to implement and are prepared to fine-tune as needed over time.

Decades ago, African American jazz singer Betty Carter challenged women everywhere with her statement: "You can do anything you want to do, if you know what to do." Now you, too, know what to do to ascertain your current status and pinpoint your goals, in the interest of managing your wealth effectively. Chapter 3 will introduce three fundamental concepts to keep you moving in the right direction.

CHAPTER 3

# Determine What
# You Need to Know

*"Constant use will not wear ragged the fabric of friendship."*

—Dorothy Parker

Most of us want to follow our hearts and at the same time do the right thing with our money so we can enjoy the style of living we prefer. Thus, being informed about fundamental financial concepts is vital. For starters, you took the time to grasp the particulars of your finances and to identify the goals you want to accomplish as you completed the previous two chapters.

With these essential elements in place, what else do you need to know to manage your wealth effectively? You need familiarity with three fundamental concepts: understanding risk, recognizing the impact of time, and aiming to profit from the power of compound returns. Familiarity with these concepts will help you prepare to construct a strong investment foundation, addressed in Chapter 4.

Understanding these three investment tenets may also help you bypass poor investment results, which lead to common investor complaints such as: "I would have *so* much more money if only I knew the best investments, if only the market had not dropped in 2008, if only investing were not so risky." In my experience, the investor's choices, not the financial markets, are usually to blame for minimal portfolio accumulation.

That being said, the way to get off the "if only" bandwagon is to determine what you need to know, as illustrated by the story of Sara and Saul. Sara and Saul both came from working-class families. Aesop's fable, "The Tortoise and the Hare," describes Sara's family's attitudes perfectly. They patiently plodded slowly and steadily towards their long-term savings goals. Saul, on the other hand, came from a family where chaos ruled the family. Money was for consumption—preferably as quickly as possible and maybe even before it was earned.

Both Sara and Saul were smart and personable people. They had no trouble doing well in college. After graduation they achieved high paying jobs in their respective fields. Before long they brought home a combined income of well over a half a million dollars each year (after taxes). Their typical way of life quickly went from no frills to high material standards. For both Sara and Saul, their combined income permitted them to become cocky about money. "We can do what we want. Why shouldn't we? We work hard." For instance, one of Saul's favorite activities was to cruise the local mall and spend about $20,000 per month (yes, per month) on items that caught his eye.

By the time Sara's uncle insisted they call me, they had dissipated 100 percent of their earnings for more than two decades. They knew they earned a lot. After all, they always fell into the highest income tax bracket. What they could not understand was why they were broke all the time.

Sara summoned up her courage and scheduled an initial consultation. With no money set aside to invest, it was premature for them to become clients. However, our initial conversation did help them begin moving in a new direction. I was able to show them how to assess their current situation. Then I was able to help them identify their goals. As our conversation unfolded, Sara and Saul admitted they only had themselves to blame for being broke all the time. They expressed confidence that rather than continuing their habit of complaining, they were ready, for the first time, to plan, invest, and think long-term.

I encouraged them to increase their savings and make an appointment to continue our dialogue when the amounts in their savings and investing buckets had grown. After they put an investment foundation in place, we could work together in applying the following fundamentals:

- Understanding risk
- Recognizing the impact of time
- Aiming to profit from the power of compound returns

As I suggested to Sara and Saul, all of us investors need to recognize each of these fundamental concepts as a friend. And since investing is a lifelong endeavor, I would go one step further. I encourage you to embrace all three—risk, time, and compound returns—as your BFF's.

## Fundamental Concepts

Thank you to teenage girls for coining the expression, BFF, which means *Best Friend Forever*. As part of your endeavor to apply fundamental principles to how you manage your wealth, consider embracing risk, time, and compound returns as your investment BFF's. Yes, we love each one.

## Risk: First BFF

When it comes to putting your money to work for you, what is the risk that you should accept? You must become comfortable with the notion that invested accounts will fluctuate. Not only will your account values fluctuate, there is no way to know when or by how much they will fluctuate.

In tandem with this fact of fluctuation, there is no way to know when you will make money or exactly how much you will make. Therefore, your profits are likely to be dynamic and somewhat unpredictable. Sound intimidating? It doesn't need to be. Remember, fluctuations in your accounts are a normal occurrence—they are neither bad nor good. Similarly, negative returns on your investment statements from time to time are also normal. They are not synonymous with a bad report card.

Take for example this illustration of Dana's experience learning about risk. Dana had recently been informed she would inherit a sizable portfolio from her mother. But what should she do with her inheritance? She knew she didn't want to take any risks. After all, she would be fifty soon and she needed this money to supplement her income. Didn't risk mean she might lose it all? She could hear her mother's voice, "A bird in the hand is worth two in the bush. A bird in the hand is worth two in the bush." That was her mother's favorite slogan in favor of choosing guaranteed interest products at her local bank—even when interest rates had sunk lower than 1%—rather than riskier products.

Clearly, Dana had received strong and limiting money messages from her parent. For starters, what she needed was a concrete framework for understanding risk. Thus, I introduced U.S. Treasury bills because they represent the most commonly cited asset offering a risk-free rate of return.[3]

I showed Dana that if she invested only in U.S. Treasury bills, she might earn about a 2% rate of return. While she could see instantly that such an investment could offer her more than the bank, she could also see it did not keep up with inflation. She had identified a big concern of investors. They not only want to stay ahead of inflation, but they also want to make money in the process.

For instance, generally speaking an investor hopes to earn at minimum:

1. The yield on Treasury's 2%, plus

2. The rate of inflation 3%, plus

3. Another couple of percent return 2%.

Stated numerically: 2% (Treasury's) + 3% (inflation) + 2% = 7% total return. Aiming to achieve a 7% total return is what investors commonly think of as being rewarded for taking risk; in other words, being

---

[3]Because the U.S. government has the authority to simply print money, there is almost no risk that those who purchase Treasury bills will not receive their interest and principal payments when due.

rewarded for putting up with fluctuating portfolios rather than settling for a U.S. Treasury bill risk-free rate of return.

Why should Dana consider accepting risk as one of her BFF's? Without taking risk, her portfolio is unlikely to grow enough to keep pace with inflation. For example, let's suppose Dana drives a car. Average gasoline prices in the year 2000 hovered around $1.50 per gallon. Ten years later, they hovered around $2.75 per gallon.

This is an example of how a person's basic living expenses can almost double in ten years. By helping Dana understand and then assume some degree of risk in her portfolio, I was preparing her to accept the need to offset the impact of inflation, not just in gasoline prices but in the prices of other basic needs as well. And by assuming some risk, Dana may also earn enough in her portfolio to have a cushion—the final 2% factor. For a woman as young as Dana, a cushion could prove crucial. After all, life is dynamic, and our needs and wants tend to change over time. For most of us, having the funding to support those changes means being able to have the style of living we prefer.

Dana and I returned to the formula: 2% (Treasury's) + 3% (inflation) + 2% = 7% total return. While it would take time and investment experience to trust the formula, and she would have to accept that there was no way to know when her portfolio value would fluctuate, aiming for a 7% outcome appealed to her. She also recognized the impact of inflation and did not want to be forced to change her lifestyle due to rising costs as the years passed.

And what if she desired more money when she retired and finally had time to travel? Having a funding cushion made good sense to her. She was now ready to revisit her late mother's mantra that regularly replayed in her mind. Dana replaced those old thoughts with her very own mantra, "Risk is my BFF."

## Didn't Everyone Lose a Lot?

Unlike Dana, long-time investors Peggy and John did not seem fearful of risk when they first contacted me. But did they understand it? They were both well into their seventies and had been retired almost ten years. They first told me their accounts had dropped over 50% in 2008. But they immediately shrugged it off with, "Didn't everyone lose a lot?" They continued to enthusiastically report their advisor was a great guy because he always reminded them that if "you take more risk, you get more return." In fact, he showed them a chart whenever they met to reassure them they would still achieve their goals, despite their ages and in spite of the 2008 debacle. While I never saw the reassuring chart provided by that advisor, I knew, due to their respective ages, that they didn't have much time left to make up for those steep portfolio downturns. And maybe they knew it, too, since they were sitting in my office and not in the office of their current advisor.

To make informed decisions and to preserve their capital, they needed a better understanding of risk. Specifically, they needed to know how much the downside impact of risk could harm their investments. Before the 2008 downturn they had about $2 million invested. When we met in 2009, their portfolios were worth just over $1 million.

As I mentioned earlier, we never know when markets are going to head up and when they are not. The first big lesson facing Peggy and John had to do with the confidence they had put in the old adage that "you take more risk, you get more return." Frankly, it ain't necessarily so. Their greatly reduced portfolio proved it. They also needed to learn that it is possible to select a portfolio asset mix of stocks and bonds that aims to limit the downside when times are tough. I introduced these rules of thumb to them so they could consider how much downturn they might be able to tolerate in their $1 million portfolio should a future market experience a correction (Figure 2).

| Asset mix | $1,000,000 portfolio | New value |
| --- | --- | --- |
| 80% stock investments | 35% drop | $650,000 |
| 60% stock investments | 25% drop | $750,000 |
| 40% stock investments | 15% drop | $850,000 |

**Figure 2:** Portfolio Asset Allocation and Market Corrections

Both Peggy and John expressed surprise at this analysis. No one had ever discussed the relationship between the proportion of stocks in their portfolio and the percentage of decrease in value likely to occur during a market correction. Particularly due to their ages, this perspective could make all the difference in preserving their investment capital going forward.

While Dana needed to understand the potential benefits of assuming capital market risk, Peggy and John needed to understand that watching one's portfolio drop into a deep, dark hole is not inevitable. They needed to learn it is possible to consider what proportion of stocks may help them avoid that outcome.

Another aspect of risk called *reversion to the mean* needs to be explored. Here is how reversion to the mean works:

1. Periods of above-average performance in the capital markets are followed by
2. Periods of below-average performance, and
3. Bad times inevitably set the stage for surprisingly good performance in the capital markets.

As you can see, reversion to the mean is as straightforward as 1, 2, 3. However, emotions intervene. Depending on how far below average the periods of below-average performance happen to be, maintaining a long-term perspective can require grit. But our investor emotions do not change the facts; they simply make it more difficult to honor the facts. As an investor, if you honor: a) the potential benefits of taking risk (Dana's formula); b) the selection of an asset allocation aimed at limiting downside risk; c) the powerful law of financial statistics, reversion to the mean, you are likely to have a positive and peaceful lifetime investing experience.

Before we dive into a discussion of time, let us turn to Benjamin Graham for some wisdom. Benjamin Graham, deemed the founder of security analysis following his publication of *The Intelligent Investor* in 1949, observed: "The investor's chief problem—and even his worst enemy—is likely to be himself."

As long ago as 1949, this world-renowned guru made it clear to us.

If we investors permit ourselves to run on emotion rather than on respect for how the capital markets work, watch out. We will probably not be happy with our results.

## Time: Second BFF

I know when I look in the mirror in the morning I am not completely convinced that time is my best friend. Instead I am reminded of Dolly Parton's remark about time. In her role as Truvy in *Steel Magnolias*, she is famous for complaining, "Honey, time marches on, and eventually you realize it is marchin' across your face."

On the other hand, as I mentioned in the Introduction, time has certainly been my friend when it comes to investing. My consistent investing year after year into a 403(b) plan has rewarded me well. As an important bonus, it permitted me to abandon career number one (teaching) and start career number two (establishing my own business).

Actually, time is integral to the definition of the word *invest*. Invest means to spend or devote for a future advantage or benefit. In other words, we choose to engage in a consistent behavior now and over a period of time because we anticipate a future reward. We invest. And the potential rewards occur over time.

Because our reward is anticipated in the future, the gratification for our consistent effort is delayed. Think back to when you were in kindergarten. How do you think you might have responded to the marshmallow test? The marshmallow test was designed to show a willingness, or not, to wait for a reward. It is used with children in kindergarten to measure each student's ability to wait or delay a reward.

Here's how it goes: Each student in the class is given one marshmallow. The children are told that the teacher needs to leave the room for a few minutes. They are told to wait to eat their marshmallow until the teacher returns. If they *do* wait, then the teacher promises them a second marshmallow upon her return.

Be honest. Would you have waited for a second marshmallow? (What if the teacher did not return in time to give you the second one?)

Or would you have gobbled up the first one the minute the teacher left the room?

The need to invest today while recognizing that reward will be delayed reflects age-old wisdom. In fact one centuries-old fable, "The Grasshopper and the Ants," illustrates the need to act even while knowing reward will be delayed and also illustrates the negative consequences procrastination can produce.

### The Grasshopper and the Ants

*All summer long a merry grasshopper spent his days making music. When he saw the ants marching past him in a line, carrying seeds and grain to store in their hill, he laughed at their toil. "How foolish, to work so hard in the hot sun!" the grasshopper cried. "Summer's the time to play and sing. There's time enough to worry about winter when the first snow falls."*

*But when the days grew short and the first snow fell, the grasshopper could find nothing to eat. Shivering in the cold, he came to ask the ants for help. "Please, can't you spare me a seed or a leaf?" he begged. "I'm too hungry even to sing!"*

*The ants shrugged in disdain. "We worked hard for our food and we have none to spare," they said. "All summer long you made nothing but music. Now all winter long you can dance!"*

# Willingness to Delay Gratification

As I have illustrated, certain practices set the stage for your portfolio to benefit from your second BFF, time. These practices include:

- Consistent investing over time
- Willingness to delay gratification
- Avoiding procrastination

Just how helpful is time to your investment gains? In simplest terms, the longer you leave your money invested before using it, the greater your account values are likely to become. This is true even if you do not add more to your portfolio. To illustrate I will use a one-time investment of $100,000.

If you are able to earn 7% on your $100,000, it may be worth $811,650 in thirty years. If you do not have thirty years before you will need to use your money, here are the values you may achieve over shorter periods of time:

$141,763 –    5 years

$200,000 –  10 years

$284,895 –  15 years

$403,874 –  20 years

$572,542 –  25 years

$811,650 –  30 years

So why don't all investors end up with impressive long-term gains? A common obstacle, especially for women, is we fear we don't know enough to make the right decisions so we procrastinate or succumb to inertia.

Perhaps we feel insecure because we are not familiar with the jargon used by industry leaders. It is intimidating to be unsure of the meaning of industry terms we hear on the news or read in the papers. For instance, terms like "bull market" and "bear market" sound so important. Let us take a moment and demystify them. First, these terms simply describe capital market conditions—over time. Second, they describe measurements of market fluctuations. And third, these "bull" and "bear" measurements are frequently presented with a good deal of drama. No wonder they sound so important.

Generally speaking, a bull market measures: *the lowest close reached after the market has fallen 20% or more—to the next high point reached by the markets.* Of course bull markets give us investors hope because we are watching markets move higher.

Generally speaking, a bear market measures: *the duration of the index closing down at least 20% from its previous high close—to the lowest close reached after the index has already fallen 20% or more.* Of course bear markets cause us fear because we are watching markets move lower without knowing when the bottom will be reached.

I imagine that wasn't too difficult to follow. But do not be surprised if the terms do not make sense the next time you hear them. This could be because these terms, like other industry jargon, are often inconsistently applied. Even experts are not necessarily consistent in their usage. No wonder it can be hard to feel confident.

When I think of the need for personal confidence, Leah comes to mind. Leah and I met just after she had come through a heart-wrenching divorce. Her twenty-year marriage had ended when her husband ran off with a younger woman, whom he married ASAP following their divorce.

During her marriage Leah had deferred all financial decision-making to her husband. She had come to assume over the years that he knew and she didn't know. Now she had a $2 million settlement. She was barely fifty years old and needed that money to last for decades. Leah felt lost. In fact she was so intimidated by the need to take charge of her financial life that she brought her nineteen-year-old son to our first meeting. She exuded tension as she entered the office. Her son, on the other hand, seemed completely at ease. He informed me with great confidence that he was thinking of studying economics in college and thought his mom could use his help.

Leah looked over at him with a proud glow on her face. When she looked back at me, she looked terrified. I began to ask her questions about her values. Before answering, she would look over at her son for reassurance. By the time we reached the goals questions, the tension in her body had begun to diminish somewhat and she stopped checking in with her son for validation before answering each question. All of a sudden Leah said, "I thought we were here for you to tell me about stocks and bonds. I thought we would have to look at all those charts my ex's financial advisor used to show us. I never understood a word he was saying.

"But you are asking me what is important to me and what I want my money to do for me. And you are explaining how risk and time can help me. I never thought about any of this before."

To her son's credit (and my surprise) he did pipe up, "Yes, Mom. She has to understand what you are trying to accomplish before she can go to work on your portfolio. She can't pick investments that are good for you unless she understands who you are."

To highlight her son's comment, not only did I need to understand what Leah hoped to accomplish, but Leah needed clarity. She needed instruction to develop familiarity with her new BFF's: risk and time. Only then might she begin to gain much-needed confidence.

## Third BFF: Compound Returns

Our third BFF is compound returns. Why do we love compound returns as much as our other two BFF's, risk and time? We love compound returns because they help our portfolios appreciate significantly over time.

Compound returns operate on a very simple principle. When you put money aside to earn returns and then reinvest those returns, you have two things working for you. Both your original investment and your returns are positioned to appreciate as time unfolds. The longer you allow this process to continue, the greater your accumulation may be.

It is the cumulative nature of compound returns that makes them our BFF. For example, let's say you invest $1,000,000. In year one you earn 8%. So now, without adding any more money, you have $1,080,000 in your portfolio as you head into year two. If you gain again in year two, your appreciation will now be cumulative—or, compounded—with your higher value of $1,080,000 as your starting point.

Naturally investors love compound returns when there are gains. But how do market downturns affect the dollars in our accounts? To illustrate this concept, a picture is worth a thousand words. Let us look closely at a couple of features of the impact of compounding in Lynn's and Cheryl's investment experience (Figure 3).

| | COMPOUND RETURNS (over time) | | | |
|---|---|---|---|---|
| | Lynn's Investment | | Cheryl's Investment | |
| Year | Rate of Return | Ending Value | Rate of Return | Ending Value |
| 1 | 8% | $1,080,000 | 30% | $1,300,000 |
| 2 | 8% | $1,166,400 | -20% | $1,040,000 |
| 3 | 8% | $1,259,712 | 25% | $1,300,000 |
| 4 | 8% | $1,360,489 | -20% | $1,040,000 |
| 5 | 8% | $1,469,328 | 25% | $1,300,000 |
| Arithmetic Return | 8% | | 8% | |
| Compound Return | 8% | | 5.39% | |

For illustration purposes only. Not a promise of a particular investment result.

**Figure 3:** Compound Returns Comparison Chart

Both Lynn and Cheryl began with a single investment of $1,000,000. Take a look at year 5 of the illustration. You will notice that Lynn's investment has appreciated to $1,469,328. Her investment compounded from $1,000,000 to $1,469,328.

Cheryl's investment, on the other hand, has appreciated to just $1,300,000. At the end of five years, she has $169,328 *less* than Lynn in her account. This is because Cheryl's aggressive investment suffered two steep downturns during this five-year period, compared to Lynn's moderate, consistently performing allocation.

Another way to understand the situation is by taking a look at this bar graph illustration of the same fact pattern (Figure 4). Cheryl (dark bar) had less money compared to Lynn (light bar), within the first five years of their respective investments of $1,000,000.

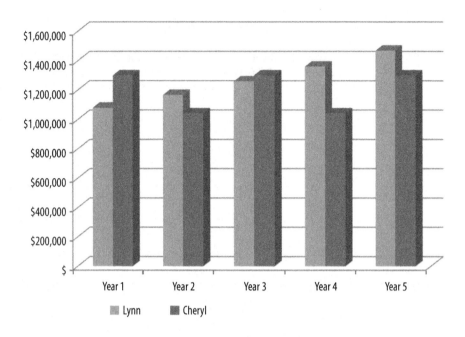

**Figure 4:** Compound Returns Comparison Bar Graph

How can these results be accurate, especially since there were three exciting years in Cheryl's portfolio? She gained 30% in year 1, 25% in year 3, and 25% again in year 5. Lynn's returns were boring. They never surpassed 8%.

As mentioned above, during two of the five investment years, Cheryl's portfolio dropped substantially compared to Lynn's. That meant she started years 2 and 4 with a much lower account value than Lynn did prior to earning positive returns. In other words, she was starting behind at the close of years 2 and 4. By comparison, Lynn's consistent returns put her account value in the lead.

Just like Cheryl, Helen and Howard had less in their portfolios instead of more. They had missed out on a lot of compound returns before we met. They reported that their initial investing experience, in the late 1990s, had been exciting. During those exciting years they had been diligent savers and investors. But their zeal dissipated as quickly as their portfolios when the twenty-first century dawned. They reported that by the beginning of 2002 they had given up their investments. They sold 100% of their holdings, converting everything to cash.

After watching markets fall in 2000 and again in 2001, Helen and Howard felt crushed. They concluded, "What difference does it make if we don't earn much? At least we aren't going down." They reported to me they felt pretty smart about that decision to move to cash as they watched markets continue to drop well into 2002.

But then, as will happen, the markets reversed course. An upward trend began in 2003. It lasted well into 2007 and provided big rewards to numerous investors. In fact, most investors like Lynn, with boring portfolios, were able to recover and make money. Helen and Howard, on the other hand, were frustrated once again because their cash portfolios earned almost nothing.

What Helen and Howard had overlooked until now was that risk, time, and compound returns could serve as their BFF's, if only they would let them. But Helen and Howard used these fundamental concepts as their best friends only during good times. When they felt like geniuses because the capital markets—and therefore their accounts—were heading straight up, they loved risk, time, and compound returns. But when markets cycled back down, they abandoned their best friends.

Thus, Helen and Howard experienced a high degree of frustration as they missed out on so much potential profit. As we have learned, BFF means *Best Friend Forever*. The forever part could have made all the difference in Howard and Helen's portfolios.

## Balancing Act Implications

As we have seen in *Determine What You Need to Know*, aiming to do the right thing with your money can be fraught with pitfalls. For instance, our friends Peggy and John did not really understand risk, which left them with substantial account losses after they had already retired. Sara and Saul ignored the potential benefits of time entirely, causing them to waste their considerable earnings for over two decades. Helen and Howard left years of compound returns on the table. And, of course, plain old procrastination and inertia can be powerful obstacles to one's intention to balance effective financial choices within the context of cherished values, needs, and interests.

What a difference it made when these individuals sought assistance. I was able to serve in the financial advisor role of "teacher." In this role I helped these clients move beyond common pitfalls when making decisions about the long-term impact of risk, time, and compound returns.

Should you need to fortify your intention to determine what you need to know to manage your wealth, consider increasing your motivation by reading this report: "Harnessing the Power of the Purse: Female Investors and Global Opportunities for Growth." The Center for Talent Innovation (www.talentinnovation.org) published it recently, and I draw your attention to one particular finding. The study indicated that affluent American women, on average, maintain 20% of their assets in cash. Therefore, in essence, 20% of their money is not working for them.

By now you know this situation need not be. It is no longer inevitable that women should leave large portions of their investment potential idle. To help you avoid such a misstep, I encourage you to complete the following exercises.

### Exercise #1: Consider Adopting Risk as Your BFF

Start by going to this address: **www.financialcalculator.org/investing/ future-value-calculator**. On the **Future Value Calculator** in the middle of the page:

1. Enter the value of your current investable assets.
2. Enter the annual rate of return to which you aspire (regardless of your current asset allocation).
3. Enter the number of years you have before you need to use your funds.

4. Hit Compute.

5. The calculator will tell you how much may accumulate in your portfolio. Make a note of the prospective accumulated portfolio value.

Now re-enter the same data for #1 and #3, but change your entry for #2. If you first selected a conservative rate of return, now select a rate of return 2% higher. If you selected an aggressive rate of return the first time, now select a rate of return 2% lower. Take note of the prospective accumulated value with the new assumed rate of return and compare it to #5 above. The differences, whether higher or lower, provide concrete examples of the potential impact of risk.

### Exercise #2: Consider Adopting Time as Your BFF

Clear your data from the Future Value Calculator in the middle of the page. Now enter your original factors. But change the number of years you originally selected in two ways:

1. Add 5 years to your original time factor and compute.

2. Subtract 5 years from your original factor and compute.

What impact do you see? You are likely seeing evidence of the impact of time as your BFF.

### Exercise #3: Consider Adopting Compound Returns as Your BFF

Start by going to this address: **www.financialcalculator.org/investing/interest-calculator**. On the **Compound Interest Calculator** in the middle of the page:

1. Enter the value of your current investable assets.

2. Enter the amount of the monthly investment you intend to make.

3. Enter your anticipated rate of return.

4. Enter the number of years during which you intend to invest.

5. Hit Compute.

6. Take a look at your expected future portfolio value.

7. And take note of your earnings—or, your compounded returns.

Every so often I run these calculations for myself because the results reaffirm my personal financial planning efforts. Even if your target date for using your investments is decades out, it can be reassuring to look concretely at your financial assumptions and targets.

Take heart, too, from Dorothy Parker's quote: "Constant use will not wear ragged the fabric of friendship." In fact, the consistent application of our BFF's—risk, time, and compound returns—with respect to investment planning is likely to provide you with ever increasing benefits as the years unfold.

# PART II

# Protect Your Lifestyle Now and in Retirement

One of the most frequently stated client financial goals is the desire to maintain their current style of living now and into retirement. I do not recall ever hearing anyone suggest that taking a step backwards would be okay, not even a little step.

In **Part I** we addressed a variety of elements that must be balanced in order to manage wealth effectively to support your style of living. To prepare the way, you ascertained your current status, identified your values and decision-making style, pinpointed your goals, established your priorities, and familiarized yourself with three basic financial concepts: risk, time, and compound returns.

In the process, I hope you developed a deeper understanding of your personal finances and gained a new level of confidence as you completed the chapter exercises. If you completed them with your spouse, I suspect you discovered that talking about financial matters with a spouse can be an emotionally charged enterprise. Perhaps you strengthened your ability to communicate and collaborate with one another.

Your experience may have called to mind the communication challenges experienced by Laura and Jerry from Chapter 1. At his age of seventy, Jerry was ready to spend some money on exactly what he wanted—a Corvette, but his ever-practical wife Laura wanted those same dollars directed to their daughter for a down payment on her first home. Both aspirations were fulfilled, but their communication required some finesse.

Now, in Chapter 4, we are ready to deepen your sense of assurance and build your repertoire of skills so you may prepare to protect your lifestyle now and in retirement. Chapter 4 will help you understand the need to construct a strong investment foundation. Chapter 5 will address important financial concerns that go beyond investing. Finally, in Chapter 6 we will probe retirement planning specifics.

Fasten your seat belt. The stories and how-to's you are about to read may prove both exciting and transformational.

# Construct a Strong Investment Foundation

*"Nothing in life is to be feared. It is only to be understood."*

—Marie Curie, physicist and chemist, and
first woman to win the Nobel Prize

Facing the need to construct a strong investment foundation can prompt a spectrum of strong feelings. The continuum of feelings may range from a fearful "You've got to be kidding me—I can't do that!" to an adventurous "Oh, well, that sounds like a good idea."

This is probably a perfect time to mention that while research and studies abound, no one has been able to establish a clear-cut connection between intelligence and smart financial choices. So if you find yourself on the "I can't do that" end of the spectrum, no worries. You may be utterly brilliant in most endeavors, just not financial ones.

I like to refer to brilliance in one endeavor but not necessarily in another as "gifts differing." This descriptor, gifts differing, comes from Myers-Briggs Type Indicator® (MBTI®). I have found it to be universally useful, such a delightfully neutral descriptor for differences in all types of circumstances.

Jane and her husband David are a perfect example of gifts differing. Highly educated and at the top of their respective professional fields, they had learned the hard way that making smart financial choices was not their gift. They were very open about this fact. Jane reported to me that she and David had recently spent some time looking at their finances. They had begun with a financial look-back, a "truth party" Jane had called it. First, they identified costly mistakes they had made over the previous decade. Second, they pinpointed their two most cherished lifestyle goals.

By the end of their truth party, Jane and David had agreed it was time to seek assistance. They felt a strong commitment to avoiding costly mistakes going forward. They also felt a strong commitment to achieving their two primary goals:

1. To send each of their daughters to the university of her choice

2. To retire in ten years

Their truth party helped them recognize that, other than balancing a checkbook, neither of them had learned much about finance when they were growing up. In fact both had been raised in homes where personal finance was defined by living paycheck to paycheck. And their parents were grateful when the family income stretched to the next payday. Neither Jane nor David wanted to return to those days.

As our conversation turned to their financial goals, Jane was quick to remind me she had little experience with investing. She said she didn't think she could be comfortable with market volatility.

I suspected Jane lacked understanding. She had made investment decisions about her 401(k) plan from time to time, but without the assurance that comes from knowing what prompted her decisions.

Although David was more comfortable with investing jargon, he lacked confidence in the investment choices he had made, as revealed by the numerous changes he had made in his retirement plan allocation over time.

For Jane and David to achieve their most cherished life goals, they needed to implement an investment plan formulated specifically for them. And for them to have complete confidence in their investment plan, they needed to understand:

1.  The rudiments of asset allocation
2.  The counterintuitive factor: lower volatility may enhance portfolio returns
3.  The strategy of keeping more of what their portfolios earned

In fact, familiarity with these three concepts is likely crucial to all investors. This chapter presents each concept in a down-to-earth manner so you can make the right decisions as you aim to construct a strong investment foundation.

## The Rudiments of Asset Allocation

When we hear the term *asset allocation*, many of us probably picture a portfolio pie chart. These pie charts are frequently used to illustrate the asset class components of a given portfolio and are favored for their ability to paint a picture, showing at a glance how many portfolio dollars are in each asset class composing a given portfolio.

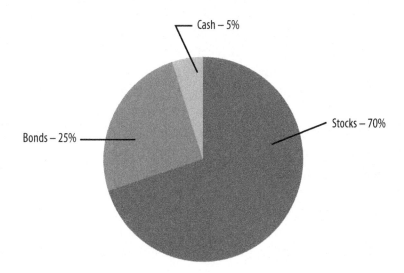

**Figure 5:** Portfolio Pie Chart

The asset class components of an individual's portfolio are, quite simply, the ingredients in the portfolio. There are three main asset classes, or ingredients: stocks, bonds, and cash.

What defines an asset class is the type of security. A stock is a type of security that represents a proportionate share of ownership of a company. A bond is a type of security that represents a loan to the government or a corporation. And cash is good old-fashioned paper currency.

Let us assume an investor is holding stocks in her portfolio. She may have purchased individual stocks, stock mutual funds, or stock exchange-traded funds (ETF's). An exchange-traded fund is a mutual fund that is traded on a stock exchange just like individual stocks are, rather than being priced once daily at the market's close each day, as stock mutual funds are.

This same investor may also hold bonds in her portfolio, and her bonds could typically be held as individual debt securities, bond mutual funds, or bond ETF's. Finally, an investor is likely to have a cash component in her portfolio. Cash is often held in a money market fund. If banking is offered by the custodian (the financial institution that keeps custody of stock certificates and other assets of a mutual fund), cash can be held in some type of bank savings or checking account vehicle.

It is useful to think of asset allocation as a recipe, one formulated to help you achieve your financial goals. And it is a recipe designed to help you live comfortably with your investment decisions.

For example, think about your favorite recipe for spaghetti sauce, or red gravy, as some call it. What are the ingredients you prefer to use? Everyone knows it is possible to make red gravy with just a few ingredients: tomatoes, salt, and perhaps some basil. But many people like to jazz it up. They want more impact from their spaghetti sauce so they add aromatic ingredients such as onions, fennel, carrots, and garlic. Finally, there are the truly adventurous who insist on adding hot peppers in their red gravy.

Using the three-ingredient red gravy metaphor, an investor formulating her investment plan may decide to assign just three asset classes in her portfolio. She may choose an asset allocation mix of stocks, bonds, and cash. But some investors are aiming for a more compelling effect.

Just as adding aromatic vegetables will make your red gravy zesty, so will adding more asset class categories enhance the flavor of your portfolio asset allocation. For example, you might add international securities, emerging market securities, and/or hard assets such as real estate to your asset allocation mix.

The red gravy metaphor I utilized for our rudiments of asset allocation discussion helped Jane and David cultivate a firm grasp of the asset classes in which they might invest. It was time to expand their conceptual understanding by taking a look at asset allocation as a powerful determinant of portfolio performance. Before proceeding, however, I encourage you to advance your understanding of asset allocation, too. Apply the knowledge you just gained to your own portfolio by turning to the end of the chapter and completing *Exercise #1*.

## Determinants of Investment Portfolio Performance

With the rudiments of asset allocation firmly in mind, it is time to review the surprising relationship between asset allocation and investment performance. Perspective was offered in a study called "Determinants of Portfolio Performance," first published in the July/August 1986 *Financial Analysts Journal*.

Gary P. Brinson, L. Randolph Hood, and Gilbert L. Beebower set out to discover what was most important to the performance of an individual's portfolio. Was it security selection? Was it market timing? Or, did the asset allocation decision make all the difference when it came to consistent performance over the long term?

Their findings became famous because the results of the study were so unexpected. The researchers had anticipated that security selection or market timing would win the day as determinants of portfolio performance. Instead, asset class selection emerged as critical, as illustrated in Figure 6.

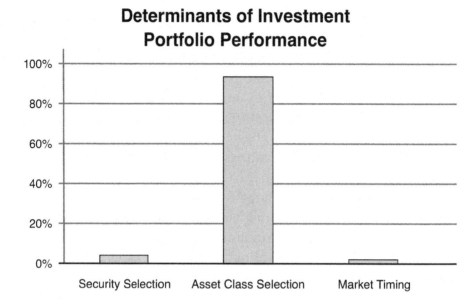

**Figure 6:** Portfolio Performance

As you can see, the impact of singular security selection and stellar market timing was negligible. Rather, it was the asset allocation decision that was crucial. The study demonstrated that the asset allocation decision investors make is likely to be the most crucial determinant of one's long-term success.

Because the results of the study were so unexpected, the decision was made to repeat the study. Brinson, Hood, and Beebower wanted to assure themselves they had controlled their factors properly; the results were the same. The authors concluded, "Because of its relative importance, investment policy (that is, asset allocation) should be addressed carefully and systematically by investors."

Although Jane and David now embraced asset allocation as a portfolio-building tool and were eager to move forward with their planning, they needed to become familiar with the notion of the counterintuitive factor before proceeding.

# The Counterintuitive Factor: Lower Volatility May Enhance Returns

The counterintuitive factor was introduced in Chapter 3 when we compared the compound returns in Lynn's portfolio after five years to the compound return performance in Cheryl's portfolio (Figure 3). You may remember Lynn's portfolio returns were higher than Cheryl's. Lynn's allocation, on the other hand, was less volatile.

According to the counterintuitive factor, if you want to enhance your returns, you may need to lower your volatility. Let us look at a simple example of this important concept. I shared the following two scenarios with Jane and David.

### Scenario 1.

Suppose you invest $1,000,000 in an all-stock portfolio and the stock market drops 50%. Now you have $500,000.

Yay! The stock market goes up 50% the following year. No, you're not out of the woods quite yet. Yes, you made 50% more, but you made 50% on just $500,000—not on your original investment.

At the end of year two, you have just $750,000. You have $250,000 less than you started with.

### Scenario 2.

Suppose you invest $1,000,000 in an allocation of mostly stock with the remainder in bonds. The stock market drops 50% but your portfolio drops only 25% because the bonds in your allocation cushioned your fall. You now have $750,000.

Yay! The stock market goes up 50% the following year. You make 35%, or $262,500 on your $750,000 account value. (Again, your gain was not 50% due to the bonds in your allocation.)

At the end of year two, you have $1,012,500 in your port-folio. This is $12,500 more than your original investment. And as you head into year three, you have $262,500 more than depicted in the preceding scenario, the **Scenario 1** all-stock allocation.

I suspect that each scenario was easy to follow. Then why do investors often overlook this knowledge when they make decisions? One reason is that industry images often mislead individuals with respect to what may happen in their portfolios from one year to the next.

For example, Peggy and John (from Chapter 3) did not anticipate steep downturns in their portfolio due to volatility. Why? Their former advisor wowed them with an asset class mountain chart (Figure 7). He

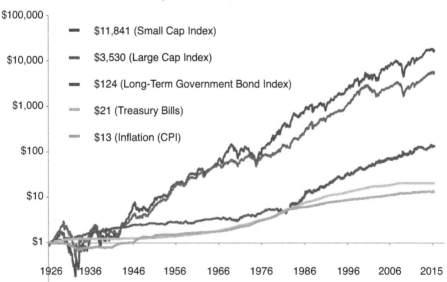

**Figure 7:** Asset Class Mountain Chart

"proved" volatility did not matter by showing his clients a chart illustrating a century of investment results, by asset class.

Take a moment and look at this chart. Think about your own portfolio. What result would you like to get? The top line? The next to the top line? Most investors want to own the asset class that does the best. However, the asset class that does the best according to this mountain chart—over a span of almost one hundred years—may not do the best next month, next year, or in the next five years.

The moral of the story is that this illustration can trap investors into ignoring the downturns in the market when deciding which assets to own. Because the image spans almost a century, the upward investment trends are more prominent than their counterpart market downturns. If, on the other hand, the illustration showed investors one year of volatility at a time, the negative impact of downturns would be much more visible.

Returning to Jane and David, they are now ready to make some decisions as they aim to achieve their two primary goals. However, before you review their process you may wish to take a moment to apply your knowledge of the rudiments of asset allocation and the counterintuitive factor to your own portfolio. I encourage you to complete *Exercise #2* at the end of the chapter.

Having completed two chapter exercises, you may wish to compare your thinking to that of Jane and David. They are considering the impact of asset allocation and the counterintuitive factor as they embark on their portfolio-building process. You may recall their two primary goals: 1) sending each daughter to the university of her choosing; 2) preparing to retire in ten years. And they have created timelines for achieving each goal.

Jane and David began by determining the appropriate level of risk for their asset allocations. This level of risk was different for each of their two primary goals, largely because of timing. For instance, the need to achieve their first primary goal was imminent. Their oldest daughter would start her freshman year of college in the fall. And their youngest would be finishing her senior year in college just before they hoped to retire, a decade from now.

The asset allocation for their college funding goal probably needed to be on the conservative side because the money they had set aside for college would be used incrementally over the next decade. And there would be little time to recover from market downturns.

As they focused on this shorter-term goal, a goal for which funds would be used within less than a year, Jane again reminded me of her discomfort with volatility. It had always scared her. To address her lingering concerns, we took a close look at the asset class mountain chart (Figure 7). In particular I drew Jane's attention to the gray line representing Treasury bills. (The returns of Treasury bills are often cited as the "risk-free" rate of return.)

One asset choice for funding their imminent need for college funds could be Treasury bills. Jane could see by looking at the gray line how negligible volatility was likely to be. She could also see that this asset barely kept pace with the gray line representing inflation. Treasury bills would not appreciate noticeably, but allocating some funds to this low volatility investment would bring her comfort. And it would make it easier for her to accept more volatility for long-term assets, their retirement funds.

With respect to their retirement funds, Jane and David decided to use three main asset classes. The asset allocation of their retirement portfolio would include stocks, bonds, and cash. They intended to allocate about 70% of their retirement funds into stocks. The remaining 30% of their portfolio would be invested in bonds and cash.

Several factors helped them decide upon this allocation. First, in a severe capital market correction, this allocation was likely to drop about 30%. They were not interested in facing a steeper downturn. Second, while they hoped to retire ten years from now, they intended to remain fully invested in the years ahead. They might not add to their portfolio after retiring, but they wanted to keep their assets working for them. Third, they intended to distribute from their portfolio at a conservative rate upon retiring. They were not certain, however, what distribution rate they should use. Longevity was a concern for both of them because they did not want to outlive their money.

## Distribution Rate from an Asset Allocation Portfolio

To help dispel their fears about outliving their money, I introduced them to the work of William Bengen. Bengen conducted definitive research on retirement distribution rates, which led to his coining the term "safe-max."

According to Bengen, safe-max is the *rate* at which income may be distributed safely from an asset allocation portfolio. His work suggests that investors using the safe-max distribution rate need not be concerned about outliving their money. However, as with all financial expectations, there are certain assumptions that must be met.

Bengen's first assumption of the safe-max distribution factor is that the asset allocation of the portfolio must have a higher proportion of stocks than bonds. His current research suggests a 65% stock component minimum in the retirement portfolio asset allocation. Secondly, Bengen assumes the investor will stick with the safe-max distribution rate. That means in the first year of income distributions, the rate should be about 4%. In subsequent years, the initial value of the income distributions may be inflation-adjusted.

Finally, Bengen's research assumes the investor will take income withdrawals for a period of thirty years. Of course that is good news for most retirees! Thirty years of retirement living has a good ring to it.

Now let us apply these assumptions[4] to Jane's and David's investment planning. They were comfortable allocating 70% of their $2 million retirement portfolio to stocks. Of the remaining 30%, 25% would be directed into bonds and 5% would be allocated to cash. Their decision to allocate 70% of their retirement nest egg to stocks fulfilled Bengen's first safe-max assumption.

---

[4]Bengen's work is being presented as an illustration, not a promise of any particular investment result. The assumptions he utilized may or may not be pertinent to your situation; it is important to consult with your professional advisors before taking action.

They would not be tested on their commitment to fulfilling Bengen's second assumption for about a decade, when they actually retired. But it is interesting to contemplate how much income they might be able to count on in ten years if they follow Bengen's assumptions.

Due to the level of risk of their asset allocation, their retirement portfolio would have a good chance of doubling over the next decade. So let's assume Jane and David's retirement portfolio accumulates to $4 million before day one of their retirement. When day one of retirement arrives, they will need to begin drawing income distributions. Having agreed with one another to stick with the safe-max distribution rate assumptions of 4%, their first annual income distribution would be about $160,000.

Their annual income distribution assumption in year two would be inflation-adjusted. If we assume a 3% inflation rate, their second annual income distribution would be approximately $164,800.

With respect to Bengen's third assumption, Jane and David certainly anticipate their longevity will be similar to their parents, who have now attained the ages of eighty-six and eighty-nine years old. They recognize, too, that their "bill" for retirement will be the largest bill of their lives. Therefore, learning about safe-max distribution rates was particularly reassuring to them.

One cautionary observation is that preparing to fund a bill of that magnitude requires not simply planning effort but also patience. In fact, patience is sometimes the hardest part. For instance, it can be challenging to remain confident you have charted the right course of action when the next-door neighbor or the media reports scintillating investment returns that could be yours—right now! ("Are mine that terrific?" you may wonder. "Am I doing the right thing?")

The next time you wonder whether you formulated the correct investment plan, take inspiration from Aesop's fable "The Tortoise and the Hare."

*A conceited hare boasted about her speed to everyone who would listen. "Not even the North Wind is as fast as I am!"*

*she declared. "No animal in the forest could beat me in a race!"*

*Now, a tortoise nearby grew tired of such bragging. "We've all heard you talk, but we've never seen you run," she said. "Why don't you race with me, and then we'll see who is the fastest."*

*The hare burst out laughing. "I could beat you standing still!" she exclaimed. But she agreed that they would race to an oak tree around a bend in the road. In an instant they were off—the hare soon out of sight, the tortoise plodding step by patient step.*

*"I've practically won already!" thought the hare as she dashed around the bend in the road. "I could stretch out here and take a little rest, and still beat that tortoise by a mile." And she settled down by the side of the road. She planned to jump up and finish the race the minute she saw the tortoise. But the grass was so soft and the sun was so warm that before the hare realized it, she had fallen fast asleep.*

*Meanwhile, the tortoise continued on. Slowly she came around the bend in the road and passed the sleeping hare. She was only a few feet from the oak tree when the hare woke from her nap.*

*Seeing the tortoise so close to the finish, the hare leaped up and tore along the road as if the hounds were after her. But she was too late. Before she could reach the oak tree, the tortoise had already been declared winner by the crowd of cheering bystanders.*

Investors who are willing to be consistent and plodding like the tortoise are more likely to achieve all their financial goals. When it comes to investing, take heart from the moral of Aesop's fable: "Slow and steady wins the race."

# How to Keep More of What Your Portfolio Earns for You

Let us assume that you have prepared well and, with patience, you are on your way to obtaining the portfolio results you want. An invisible obstacle may be present that could blindside your investment results. This obstacle is the costs associated with being an investor. Therefore, in addition to careful preparation, you have another task—determining how to retain the maximum amount of what your portfolio earns for you.

How does one aim to retain portfolio earnings? Investors may keep more of their portfolio profits by minimizing the costs associated with investing. Common costs include:

- Commissions
- Mutual fund operating expenses
- Income taxes

Costs such as these mentioned are subtracted from what you get to keep. For instance, once upon a time an investor had to pay steep commissions when buying or selling a security. The fees ate away at investor earnings. Now such commissions are generally discounted or negligible.

Investors purchasing mutual funds need to pay attention to internal costs such as fund operating expenses. These costs can vary widely, sometimes according to the objective of a particular fund. For example, international funds usually cost more to operate than domestic funds because they require management teams to interface with global currencies when purchasing international securities. This additional behind-the-scenes work leads to higher operating expenses.

## Taxes Often Reduce Portfolio Results

For most of us, income taxes are the biggest hindrance to keeping portfolio earnings. As our investments appreciate in value, our earnings are usually taxed at the federal and state levels depending on the rules of the state in which one resides.

Annual income taxes on investment gains can be confusing. But before taking a closer look I want to remind you that most retirement plans are tax-deferred. Accounts that are tax-deferred do not require you to pay annual taxes on gains. When you begin to spend from your retirement account or when you attain the age at which you are required by the tax code to begin distributions, however, your distributions are likely to be 100% state and federally income taxable. Again, state rules vary.

A discussion of Sybil's experience helps illustrate how insidious annual income taxes on investments can be. We began working together not long after her acrimonious divorce was finally settled. Her late brother had advised her in the past, but now she needed a new relationship. When we met, Sybil indicated a preference for retaining only one of her current portfolio strategists, the one her late brother had favored, even though that particular strategist traded heavily each year. Notably, it was not uncommon for that investment manager to trade 100% of Sybil's securities in that account every year.

This behavior is often referred to as 100% turnover in a portfolio. If Sybil was determined to retain that strategist, she could anticipate having to pay hefty capital gains tax bills year after year. Those liabilities would be levied in addition to tax bills accrued for dividends or interest she had earned.

To assist Sybil in preparing for the decisions she would ultimately have to make, I introduced her to another investment strategist, one that had a competitive performance similar to the current one but a different trading philosophy. In other words, I introduced her to a strategist who typically trades 10% of an investor's securities annually instead of 100%. Next, as part of our due diligence, we conducted a conference call with the original strategist. One of that firm's managers admitted the taxes resulting from all those trades diminished investor returns by 3–4% annually.

For a moment let us think about the implications of that phone call. Suppose performance is diminished by 3% per year and a loyal investor retains the strategist for a decade. Accordingly, 30% of her profits will evaporate into taxes. Generally speaking, a 30% reduction of investment gains for ten years is attention-getting.

You do not need to be an accountant to know that a portfolio with 100% turnover each year is almost certain to trigger higher annual tax bills than a portfolio with only 10% turnover annually. If you feel agitated as you read this section about tax bills, you are not alone. Most of us feel discomfort, fear even, when we examine the impact of tax consequences.

Like Sybil, you may have misgivings about making changes for sentimental reasons or because you prefer to avoid painful truths. Whatever the situation may be, I encourage you to persevere. In Sybil's case, her alternative was to choose a strategist with equivalent performance but low turnover. Therefore her future tax consequences would likely be negligible rather than hefty.

I am pleased to report Sybil was ultimately able to set aside sentiment and recognize the importance of choosing a strategist with equivalent performance data to the one her brother had favored, but one with low turnover. She made the decision to change strategists so she could reposition her investment in order to keep more of what she earned.

## Balancing Act Implications

Constructing a strong investment foundation is frequently the lynchpin of planning designed to protect our style of living now and into retirement. And the strength of this investment foundation is predicated upon your asset allocation decision, your consideration of the counterintuitive factor, and the thoroughness of your efforts to retain the maximum amount of your portfolio earnings.

As in previous chapters, the concepts you must incorporate for success interact with one another. You face the considerable task of balancing your primary goals within the context of your timelines for achieving each, comfort with risk, financial resources, and need for income distributions, to name a few.

This balancing act is complicated and probably best managed by a financial advisor serving the role of investment architect. In her role as architect, the financial advisor is responsible for constructing a strong investment plan as the foundation of your financial house. From this foundation, wealth management strategies are formulated to match your comfort with risk to your lifelong goals.

Test your ability to balance several elements required for your success building a strong investment foundation by completing the following four exercises.

### Exercise # 1: Current Asset Allocation

- Select one recent investment statement.
    - Try to determine the asset allocation proportions of your portfolio.
    - Next, calculate in a 25% market decline—which typically happens once every five years or so—by how many dollars your account is likely to decline.
    - Is this dollar decline more or less than you expected?
- Select three investment statements.
    - Try to determine the asset allocation shown on each statement.
    - Is the asset allocation for each portfolio similar or different?
    - Were you aware of the similarities or differences?

**Table to assist with Exercise #1:**

| Asset Mix | $1,000,000 Portfolio | New Value |
|---|---|---|
| 80% stock investments | 35% drop | $650,000 |
| 60% stock investments | 25% drop | $750,000 |
| 40% stock investments | 15% drop | $850,000 |

### *Exercise # 2: Comfortable Asset Allocation*

Review the above table. Based upon how much market decline you feel comfortable with, write down the asset allocation you believe makes sense for you.

Select just one account that you identified for Exercise #1. Map out the revisions to the current asset allocation that are needed, to adjust that portfolio to an asset allocation with which you feel more comfortable.

### *Exercise #3: Implement a Revised Asset Allocation*

Based upon possible costs, such as potential tax consequences (a conversation with your Certified Public Accountant (CPA) might be appropriate here), determine a schedule for updating your newly established asset allocation proportions in the account identified for revisions in Exercise #2.

For example, a schedule for implementing new asset allocation proportions might span two years or more:

> Year 1: Trade half of your account into your new asset allocation.
>
> Year 2: Trade the remainder into your new asset allocation proportions.

*Or*

> Year 1: Trade one quarter of your account into your new asset allocation.
>
> Year 2: Trade one quarter of your account into your new asset allocation.
>
> Year 3: Trade one quarter of your account into your new asset allocation.
>
> Year 4: Trade the remainder into your new asset allocation proportions.

You get the idea. Again, remember to consult with your CPA to confirm opportunities to minimize tax consequences as you update your asset allocation.

### Exercise #4: Approximate Income Distribution

Select one account that you identified for Exercise #1, from which you anticipate taking distributions upon retirement. Based upon the safe-max assumptions presented earlier in this chapter, determine approximately how much income you could take for your first year of retirement.

I hope it was refreshing to complete the exercises. If you are like me, understanding triumphs over fear every time when it comes to making financial decisions. And as the remarkable Marie Curie stated more than a century ago, "Nothing in life is to be feared. It is only to be understood." Take inspiration from her perspective as you discover in the next chapter the financial understanding you need, which goes beyond investing.

CHAPTER 5

# Secure Your
# Financial Independence

*Rich people plan for three generations;*
*poor people plan for Saturday night."*

— Gloria Steinem

Upon becoming a financial advisor in the late 1990s my biggest surprise was learning how devastating mistakes can be and how they can happen to anyone, regardless of the depth of their financial resources. From the start I was permitted to hear stories that sent that message home. The devastating mistakes I witnessed were those that affect aspects of one's financial life that go beyond investing.

Subsequent experience has taught me that no matter how carefully an investor constructs a strong investment foundation, if there are gaps in planning for financial concerns that go beyond investing, watch out! Efforts to secure financial independence are likely to end up compromised—if not immediately, then at some point in the future.

Consider what happened in 2008. Our global economy fell off a cliff. It was an economic disaster. Tens of thousands of competent professionals, at all levels, found themselves out of work. For those who never thought they would be without work, a state of shock ensued. Ready or not, they quickly learned the potential for job loss is a major financial risk for today's professionals.

The risk of job loss is no longer limited to incompetence or not getting along with the boss. It is often about factors out of our control. For example, one senior executive client who had worked for a major corporation for more than two decades suddenly learned the company had decided to sell off her division. Then an arbitrary decision was made to eliminate annual bonuses. Not surprisingly, the corporate buzz instantly became, "How long before we (employees) become history, too?"

Becoming suddenly unemployed can be catastrophically expensive for professionals. However, professionals are not the only group that faces the uncertainty of potentially catastrophic expenses. For instance, many retirees face the economic wild card of rising health care costs. Especially with today's longevity, these costs are a major concern. None of us knows how long we will live, nor whether we will be healthy or someday need long-term health care not covered by our insurance provider.

Loss of one's job and long-term health care costs are but two examples of the need to prepare for substantive financial concerns that go beyond investing. Sound complicated? It is complicated and there are a variety of elements to balance, so let me break it down into chunks. I suggest you adopt the following four categories to help you conceptualize the various aspects your wealth management needs beyond investing:

1. Wealth enhancement
2. Wealth transfer
3. Wealth protection
4. Charitable giving

This chapter will help you prepare your roadmap for categories one and two, wealth enhancement and wealth transfer. Wealth protection and charitable giving will be addressed separately in Chapters 7 and 8. We begin with an examination of the experience of Christel and Tony, whose story illustrates how important it is to think beyond your investment planning.

## Wealth Enhancement

Unknowingly, Christel and her husband Tony were not on track to secure their financial independence because they had focused solely on investing until their eldest child, their son, headed off to college. As he entered his freshman year, the passing years came into sharp focus. They realized they had given little substantive thought to preparing for their years post-young children. It seemed unbelievable they were already on the cusp of becoming empty-nesters. Suddenly Christel and Tony had questions and they wanted answers. Was their longstanding sense of pride in their investment planning well-founded? What else did they need to do to build a solid financial foundation for the years ahead?

During our discovery meeting, they shared their empty-nesters vision with me:

> Christel and Tony wanted a comfortable lifestyle. It had been well over twenty years since they had needed to scrimp and scrape to makes ends meet. Neither one had any interest in repeating that experience; they had worked too hard.
>
> They hoped to retire early and pursue other interests. To fulfill this early retirement aspiration they lived modestly and set aside money aggressively. Status as defined by material goods was not their goal. Instead, their goal was to have the financial freedom to do what they wanted, when they wanted.
>
> Christel and Tony also wanted to be in a position to help family members if the need arose in the future. They were uncertain, for instance, how well prepared their respective parents were to handle potential long-term health care costs as they aged.

When I mentioned the concept of wealth enhancement strategies, they became curious. Hadn't they already accomplished wealth enhancement by saving and investing and increasing their wealth? When I asked, "Does your portfolio aim to produce the best possible returns consistent with your level of risk tolerance?" they were uncertain. They did not know how to describe the level of risk of their invested assets.

I then asked, "What strategies have you implemented to minimize the impact of taxes?" They responded that they let their accountant think about taxes. "Another consideration is your wages and consulting fees," I continued. "As successful professionals, what strategies have you implemented to reduce the annual taxes on those earnings?" I indicated to them that the wealth enhancement aspect of securing their financial independence might be defined as: *Maximize what you earn and keep as much as possible of what you earn.*

**Maximize what you earn and keep as much as possible.**

I suspect such considerations sound self-evident, but not all of us keep them in mind. What might hold us back? For one thing, bad feelings prompt us to avoid these considerations. Take taxes, for example. Any discussion of wealth enhancement inevitably leads to a consideration of income tax consequences. And as we learned previously, discussions about taxes can arouse powerful negative emotions.

Some of us hate taxes. Others view them as inevitable social capital, but question the government's spending decisions regarding the tax dollars assessed. Other bad feelings may be aroused simply because of the time involved in organizing documents. We may feel frustrated because tax liabilities are a moving target. For example, regulations change. Opportunities to minimize taxes change. Efforts to do the right thing can be confusing. Add to that mix the fact that while tax minimization may be vital to wealth enhancement, tax minimization is rarely the end game.

## Keep More of Your Investment Profits

It did not take long for Christel and Tony to realize that evaluating their personal finances for wealth enhancement opportunities could help them fortify the financial independence to which they both aspired. They decided to begin by revisiting their investment planning. The first step was to confirm their investment returns were on track considering the level of risk with which they were comfortable; in other words, they confirmed their returns were consistent with their risk tolerance, thereby answering one of the initial questions I posed.

Reassured that their current investment strategy was appropriate, Christel and Tony turned next to the identification of income tax reduction opportunities. Like Sybil in Chapter 4, they recognized a past investment decision that had led to excessive portfolio turnover. Fine-tuning their portfolio to minimize turnover set the stage for a reduction in their annual income tax bill.

They also realized that some trading of specific asset classes in their portfolio allocation would be needed from time to time—taxes or no taxes. This trading, often called *rebalancing*, would be necessary to keep their carefully selected asset allocation on track. Christel and Tony wanted to maintain their portfolio proportions to help manage their risk, and acknowledged that rebalancing assets helped accomplish this.

Before taking action and rebalancing this year, I suggested they contact their CPA for an analysis of their probable tax consequences. In the past, their natural take-charge personalities had led them to take action before seeking advice.

The fact pattern Christel and Tony presented to their CPA included:

- The international component in their portfolio had greatly appreciated.

- They needed to trim their international position to maintain the desired level of portfolio risk.

- They wanted an estimate of the taxes that would be triggered by the sale of part of their international position.

- They had recently sold their rental property.

- They wanted an estimate of the taxes likely to be triggered by the gains from the sale of their rental property.

To avoid an excessive income tax liability, their CPA recommended they stage the selling of their international position over a two-year period. The proposed game plan involved trimming half of the international asset class position this year and waiting until the following year to trim or rebalance the other half. Because the gains on their property sale had to be reported this year, staging their portfolio rebalancing over two years made sense to Christel and Tony. And this decision saved them from two costly outcomes when they filed on April 15th: They were saved 1) from triggering premium taxes (excess federal taxes assessed when income surpasses certain thresholds); and 2) from bumping up into a higher income tax bracket.

As you can see, the concept of wealth enhancement has numerous components. So far Christel and Tony have addressed portfolio turnover and the timing for portfolio rebalancing (with the help of their CPA). As a result of engaging in this kind of analysis, Christel and Tony were able to keep more of what they had earned; they were achieving wealth enhancement.

Next, they chose to take a look at their college expenses commitment. Faced with paying college expenses for their son immediately and for their daughter in a couple of years, Christel and Tony were eager to learn about tax minimization opportunities. I introduced them to two tax-sensitive college-funding options to consider; purchasing a pre-paid college tuition plan for their son and funding a 529 plan for their daughter.

The purchase of a pre-paid college tuition plan might eliminate future income taxation on funds they had set aside for their son's education. And the aggressive funding of a 529 plan for their daughter might result in tax-free growth until her higher education expenses needed to be paid. I reminded them that tax-sensitive options such as these come with many regulations that must be honored in order to maintain the tax advantages.

Explore these and other options for yourself online: **http://www. savingforcollege.com**.

## Keep More of Your Earned Income

Just like Christel and Tony, your family may be able to keep more of what your portfolio earns through tax-sensitive decision-making. If you are an employed professional, opportunities to keep more of your earned income may be available to you, too. These often come in the form of long-term incentive (LTI) plans. Common employer-provided and self-employed opportunities include:

- Contributing the maximum to your tax-deferred retirement plan
- Contributing to a SEP IRA as well, if you have consulting income outside of your W-2 earnings
- Setting aside the maximum allowable in your employer's deferred-compensation plan
- Making a tax-deductible contribution to a qualified health savings account
- Taking advantage of employer long-term incentive (LTI) programs that enable you to defer income or control in what year you receive it
- Substituting appreciated securities for cash when making charitable contributions

Not surprisingly, employer plans vary. During annual enrollment periods, be sure to review what your current enrollment is. Compare that to your eligibility. Take note of the vesting period for selected benefits. Determine whether or not you are taking full advantage of the plans for which you are eligible and consider fine-tuning your current enrollment, if appropriate.

Christel, Tony, and I reviewed their long-term incentives (LTI's) together. We discovered three employer-provided opportunities to increase their plan participation:

- Increase contributions to their tax-deferred retirement plans to the annual maximum allowable.
- Take full advantage of their employer's qualified (tax-free) health savings account plans.
- Contribute to their deferred compensation plans.

Several positive outcomes were anticipated, including a reduction in annual income taxes while increasing their funding for early retirement.

Remember, as with college savings planning, long-term incentive (LTI) plans come with plenty of regulations. It is important to seek advice and understand the pros and the cons before implementing your decisions. Above all, you do not want to end up with a *schlimmbesserung*—an improvement that makes things worse.

You may be struck by how complicated wealth enhancement can be. Perhaps it will be easier to implement your game plan if you start with a roadmap like I prepared for Christel and Tony. The illustration in Figure 8 is their first iteration as we worked to formulate their plan for wealth enhancement.

Christel and Tony used a color code, indicated at the bottom of their roadmap, to keep themselves on track. Using their electronic version, they simply colored the completed plan components using turquoise, the in progress components in yellow, and their future action items in green. The color code shows timelines at a glance and can serve as a quick reminder of what to do now. Remember, not all aspects of your wealth enhancement plan need to happen at the same time.

Your wealth enhancement strategies may help you eliminate gaps as you plan for financial concerns that go beyond investing, thus helping you secure your financial independence. The theme of wealth enhancement will be expanded in Chapter 6 as we specifically address the needs of retirees.

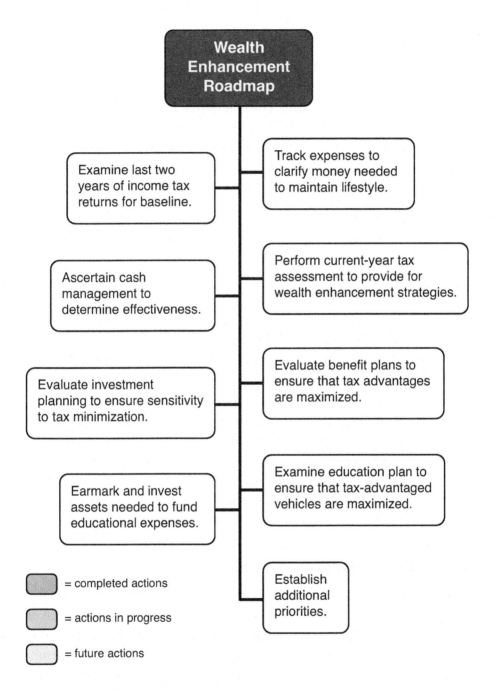

**Figure 8:** Wealth Enhancement Roadmap

# Wealth Transfer

Now it is time to turn to the second category of planning to fulfill wealth management needs, wealth transfer. Perhaps you noticed that it was important to tap into your network of professionals—your financial advisor, your CPA, and your employer human resources (HR) specialists—as you framed and implemented your wealth enhancement strategy. The assistance of a team of professionals can be invaluable. It is likely you will need to tap into this network of professionals as you address wealth transfer, too. In essence, wealth transfer planning means to *memorialize your wishes*. The assistance of your estate attorney may be crucial as you prepare.

## Memorializing Your Wishes

Even though wealth transfer sounds simple, there is a tricky part that prevents more than half of American adults from planning or implementing a plan. The difficulty involves being able to consider and accept what will happen to your loved ones and your assets when you are no longer here.

Understandably, you probably prefer not to think about dying. But if you do not plan, you will forfeit the chance to memorialize your wishes. You will forfeit the chance to be in charge. And remember, the state in which you reside has an estate plan all ready for you. The state's plan might not be anything like what you would have chosen, but it will dictate what will happen to your assets.

## Taking Care of Your Loved Ones

One family with whom I work is a model of wealth transfer preparation. Their motivation for planning was to make provisions for the care of their special needs son. Like so many families today, their adult son is afflicted with Asperger syndrome, a condition on the autism spectrum. He graduated from college, has a decent, full-time position, and is loved by his employers because he is extremely reliable and predictable.

Nevertheless, his parents still need to run interference for him from time to time. He will never be entirely self-sufficient. Their first wealth transfer task was to be certain there was someone in place ready to advise him should they no longer be able to intercede. They were fortunate to find the perfect local organization to assist.

Their second wealth transfer task was to establish a testamentary special needs trust for their son. A testamentary trust is memorialized within an individual's will and triggered upon death. These clients selected the special needs trust wrapper because it would not interfere with eligibility, should their son ever be entitled to public benefits. An outright gift or inheritance could make him ineligible for such benefits.

Our wealth enhancement discussion addressed the negative impact of income taxes. As you prepare for wealth transfer, you need to consider current rules regarding federal estate taxes, state inheritance taxes, and gift taxes, as well as the impact of income taxes. The rules and thresholds for all are, not surprisingly, a moving target, which therefore necessitates a periodic review of your documents. You want to be certain that despite changes in the tax code and other laws, your documents remain effective.

All this talk of death and taxes reminds me of the old adage, "Nothing is certain but death and taxes." But I must add a footnote. If you plan ahead for wealth transfer, the amount your family loses to taxes at your passing may be minimized.

The following story illustrates the extremely negative financial consequences that can result from a family's *un*willingness to prepare:

> The family was wealthy. Their net worth exceeded $25 million, and so they met the definition of ultra-high net worth. But dad hated attorneys and mom hated taxes so they did not plan ahead. Besides, they maintained the belief they were not going to die anytime soon.
>
> As a result of not planning, when they died, the family's ultra-high net worth status evaporated into estate and other tax liabilities.

For instance, because they did not plan for wealth transfer, $14 million of their family estate worth $25 million was subject to federal estate taxation. This meant their family owed the federal government a tax bill of around $7 million. And that was just the beginning.

Had this family prepared for wealth transfer (memorialized their wishes) with the right team of professionals, they might have saved their family literally millions of dollars at their passing. And I feel certain the Internal Revenue Service was not one of the charitable causes they had intended to benefit with all those millions of tax dollars.

As you can now clearly see, addressing tax minimization may be tedious and may engender negative emotions, but the positive consequences of such planning can be substantive. Taking the time to address your wealth transfer needs may help your family pay less in taxes when assets are transferred and, most importantly, ensure that your wishes are honored at your passing. In other words, preparing for wealth transfer may prove instrumental in helping you avoid devastating mistakes.

## Passing Assets to Your Heirs

Ultra high-net worth or not, you will probably need to complete certain wealth transfer tasks such as executing or updating your basic legal documents. Basic legal documents usually include a will, a durable power-of-attorney, a health care power-of-attorney, a living will, and perhaps a living trust. There are a number of types of trusts that serve various purposes. One example is the previously mentioned special needs trust. The topic of trusts will be more fully addressed when we discuss retirement in Chapter 6.

Contrary to what many people assume, not all assets pass by will regardless of the language in your will. For example, certain account registrations as well as beneficiary designations supersede your will. Don't make the mistake of underestimating the power of either.

Here are two stories I wish were not true. They illustrate the power of your beneficiary designation and your account registration choices:

1. Beneficiary designations matter—

    A young woman began her career, and her employment package included a pension. She named her mother as sole beneficiary since she was still living at home. As time passed, this woman did not revisit her beneficiary designation.

    After all, she was still young even if she was now married with two small children. Then suddenly, she died from cancer at the age of 38.

    Not only was it tragic that her family received no benefit from the sixteen years she had contributed to her pension, but her mother was in a nursing home now, and the facility got every dime of the young woman's pension benefit.

2. Account registrations matter—

    Sandy's husband of twenty-seven years had just died. All that was left of her family was her twenty-two-year-old daughter and herself. Of course there were one or two cousins out there, too, but they had never been close. "What a lonely place to be," she thought. "I really miss him."

    Before long, life insurance proceeds arrived in the mail—a check for $750,000. "Wow, that seems like a lot of money," Sandy thought. "I don't know if I want to invest it or just keep it safe in the bank."

    "For right now maybe I should deposit $250,000 in three different banks, so each deposit will be FDIC insured. That would bring me comfort, something I can actually count on for the future."

While driving to the first bank, Sandy decided it made sense to put the funds in a joint account with her daughter. After all, her daughter would inherit the funds someday anyway. She chose the JTWROS (joint tenants with rights of survivorship) account registration. This registration made them each a full owner of the account with access to the funds in the account.

Sandy was satisfied with her decision for some time. Then she incurred a major bill. She needed to replace her roof. Off she went to the bank to take the money she would need from one of her accounts.

Sandy was in for a shock. Her original deposit of $250,000 had shrunken to $7,000. "How can this be?" she asked. The bank associate informed her that because her account registration was JTWROS, the other person on the account had withdrawn funds from time to time, and now only $7,000 remained.

As these examples illustrate, the consequences of your wealth transfer decision-making may prove irreversible.

These stories prompted Christel and Tony to review their retirement account beneficiary designations. They were chagrined to discover the potential consequence of having named their children as contingent beneficiaries. Should they die in a mutual tragedy, their children would become account owners of large sums of money; as each child attained the age of eighteen the money would be theirs to do with as they wished.

Because this was not the outcome they intended, they contacted their attorney. Specifically, they added language to their wills so a testamentary trust would be triggered in the case of a mutual tragedy. The testamentary trust included the naming of a trustee as well as a schedule for the ages at which their children would take control of some portion of their inheritance.

However, the task was not yet completed because they still needed to update their beneficiary forms to memorialize their intent. Therefore, their attorney provided them with specific language referencing their wills, to use in updating their contingent beneficiary forms. Finally, Christel and Tony completed new beneficiary forms for each of their retirement accounts and filed them with the appropriate financial institution. Now their beneficiary forms would accomplish their intent.

By now I am sure it is clear that strategizing with care for wealth transfer can be just as complicated as it was to plan your wealth enhancement strategies. Thus, preparing a wealth transfer roadmap may be crucial as you plan to address your family's concerns. The wealth transfer roadmap seen in Figure 9, formulated for our clients with the special needs son, provides you with an example to stimulate your thinking.

As Christel and Tony did with their wealth enhancement diagram, this family stayed on track by using a color code to track their progress and also to remind them of what actions were still needed and when. Before proceeding to the next section, I cannot overemphasize the fact that few of us have the objectivity, patience, or expertise to deal effectively with matters such as those mapped on Figure 9 (page 92) or earlier in the chapter (Figure 8) without the assistance of a coordinated team of competent professionals.

## Holistic Wealth Management Process

The chapter began with the thesis that devastating mistakes can happen to anyone, regardless of the depth of their financial resources. In fact, they are likely to happen to anyone who has addressed investment planning to secure their financial independence but who stopped there. Experience has taught me investment planning is not the end game; it is the beginning. Individuals who overlook financial concerns that go beyond investing—and there may be many—are likely to be blindsided by extremely costly mistakes as the years pass.

Emily and Dan from Chapter 1 offer a perfect example. You may remember that upon inheriting a substantial portfolio of money, they

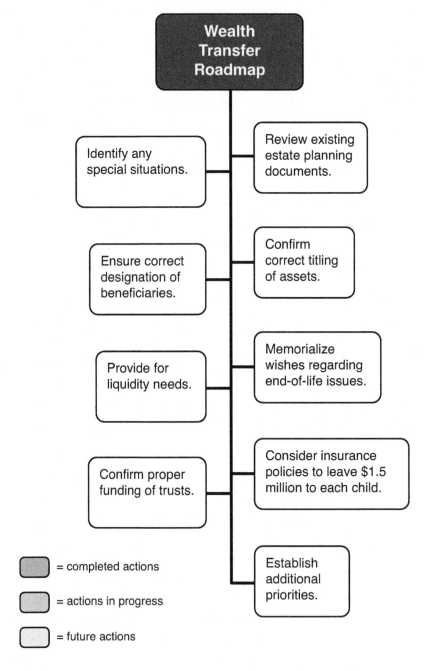

**Figure 9:** Wealth Transfer Roadmap

assumed they were set for life. But they inadvertently overlooked their family's financial concerns that went beyond investing—promised payment of expensive college tuitions, long-term care expenses for a parent, private, unreimbursed therapist expenses for their children, to name a few. Before they contacted me they had already dissipated about $2 million in a short period of time. And the money hemorrhaging continued until we were able to address their multiple financial concerns.

Within the very first month I worked as a financial advisor in 1997, I could see that no matter how astute my investment recommendations, if gaps existed in planning for financial concerns beyond investing (like in the case of Emily and Dan), investments might not ultimately be used for the intended goals. Thus, it would be difficult if not impossible for clients to achieve what was most important to them. In other words, if I limited my recommendations to just one element of wealth management—investment planning—rather than offering my clients a complete system for addressing their financial concerns, it was unlikely their goals would be satisfied.

The nature of something "holistic" is to deal with whole or complete systems rather than to dissect into individual parts. I believe true wealth management does just that. It balances the elements of a holistic system beginning with investment planning as the foundation of a client's financial house; from there it addresses concerns that go beyond investing. With the help of a team of professionals, personalized strategies are created to fulfill wealth enhancement, wealth transfer, wealth protection, and charitable giving needs.

It is probably self-evident that holistic wealth management is complicated and not a simple undertaking. That may be why only a minority of financial advisors provide this approach. For instance, although the term wealth management may have been popularized due to the status it conveys, fewer than seven percent of financial advisors utilize a holistic wealth management process. Rather, the financial services landscape has remained virtually unchanged over the years, with the vast majority of advisors trying hard to sell investment products—not to address affluent investors' complex financial needs.

There may be no better way to sum up the need affluent clients have for holistic wealth management than with Gloria Steinem's wry observation: "Rich people plan for three generations; poor people plan for Saturday night." Intergenerational planning is not about a product sale. It is about the balancing act of addressing complex financial needs today with an experienced perspective regarding what the future may hold.

## Balancing Act Implications

Wealth enhancement and wealth transfer are two aspects of planning required to secure your financial independence, in concert with your solid investment foundation. Consideration of opportunities for wealth enhancement focus on maximizing what you earn and keeping as much of what you earn as possible—portfolio profits and earned income, for example. Wealth transfer planning needs can feel particularly intimidating because decisions must be made about what will happen to your assets as well as your loved ones upon your passing. But because events occur that we cannot control—the economic crisis of 2008 leading to massive job loss, health care costs upon retirement, and ever-changing rules regarding tax consequences, to name a few—preparation is likely your best defense for avoiding expensive mistakes.

By now I am certain it comes as no surprise that to assist with this preparation, affluent clients need an independent financial advisor who approaches their personal finance needs from a holistic wealth management perspective, eschewing the traditional product-sale mindset.

My firm, Entrust Financial LLC®, has a long-standing commitment to providing independent, holistic advice, and therefore we established our firm as a fee-based independent firm. To learn more about what our approach could mean for you and your family, reach out today: 610-687-3515 or **info@entrustfinancial.com**. I would be thrilled to hear your story and to begin a dialogue regarding how we might assist.

Now I encourage you to apply what you have learned about securing your financial independence to your own personal situation by completing Exercises #1 and #2.

### *Exercise #1: Pressing Issues: Wealth Enhancement and Wealth Transfer*

- Write down the single most pressing issue you face with respect to wealth enhancement.
- You may wish to refer to the Wealth Enhancement Roadmap (Figure 8) presented earlier in the chapter.
- Write down the single most pressing issue you face with respect to wealth transfer.
- For guidance you may wish to refer to the Wealth Transfer Roadmap (Figure 9) presented earlier in the chapter.
- Now determine the appropriate professionals to assist you in addressing each of these pressing issues. Contact them today.

### *Exercise #2: Personal Wealth Enhancement and Wealth Transfer Roadmaps*

Find the downloadable Chapter 5 *Personal Wealth Enhancement* and *Personal Wealth Transfer* mapping illustrations under the **Resources** tab, **Balancingactbook.com**. Download the mapping illustrations and begin formulating your game plan for addressing your wealth enhancement and wealth transfer needs. Step-by-step instructions are provided.

Now that you are well on your way to securing your financial independence, we will look closely at what you need to do to affirm that your financial house is in order for your retirement years. Strategies presented are designed to help you protect yourself, whether you have already retired or are preparing to do so.

CHAPTER 6

# Delineate a Retirement Plan

*"I've been poor and I've been rich, and rich is better."*

—Bessie Smith

There may be few times in life when it is more important to be rich than when you retire. Think about it for a moment. Retirement will probably be the biggest bill of your life, especially with today's longevity. So it is essential to prepare ahead of time. Whether your wealth was earned, was inherited, or came as the result of a divorce settlement, retirement is not the time for guessing how much you might need. Transitioning into retirement is the time when you may have but one chance to get the economics correct.

Putting your financial house in order to prepare for retirement may prompt financial fears. A common fear is that you will run through your savings and investments too quickly. Another is that you will simply run out of money. These fears also affect stay-at-home moms who have depended on their spouse for income and retirement funding, as well as professional women accustomed to fending for themselves.

Interestingly, a stay-at-home mom named Lydia voiced some of the most strident complaints I have ever heard regarding fear of her husband's imminent retirement. There was no evidence Lydia and her husband had ever lived a life with any economic hardship. But that did not diminish her fear surrounding their retirement years, which came through loud and clear in casual conversation. What's more, it prompted Lydia to launch into a ten-minute tirade at a women's luncheon against a schoolteacher friend of hers. "Why should *she* have a pension? Why should our tax dollars help fund a pension for *her* when *we* don't have one?"

In essence, she was vexed that her husband had not earned a pension as part of his career benefits. "If he didn't have a pension, then no one else should have a pension either." Lydia's fear was abundantly evident. However, there was no evidence she understood what was driving her emotion.

Self-awareness and an understanding of certain life-cycle facts can make all the difference as you prepare for retirement. This chapter offers you a way to look at your own situation without fear. More specifically, this chapter aims to help you envision your retirement lifestyle and offers an understanding of how to prepare financially to fund and protect the lifestyle you envision. Additionally, it offers guidance in preparing for potential long-term health care expenses, too.

Finally, this chapter will help you answer some important questions regarding the retirement lifestyle you envisioned:

- How would you like to spend your time?
- How have you prepared to fund your retirement years?
- How might you set the stage to retire gracefully?

Jennifer's story serves as a springboard for our discussion. Her willingness to learn led to growing self-awareness, despite her multi-faceted situation. In contrast to Lydia, her strong need to move beyond fear motivated Jennifer to take the necessary steps for a graceful passage into retirement.

## Jennifer's Story

When we first met, Jennifer was a loyal employee of a major corporation. She had begun working for this firm upon graduating from high school, and they had paid for her college education. Meanwhile, she had steadfastly worked her way up the corporate ladder one rung at a time while raising two children.

Our meeting was serendipitous. Both of us had been invited to a social event late in 2006 and struck up a conversation at that event. She perked up when she discovered I was a financial planner. Within seconds she bubbled over with concerns about her pension. She had been funding it since starting to work at the corporation more than thirty years ago. Now according to the corporate buzz, benefits might no longer be fully paid. The thought horrified her. Furthermore, employees with tenure such as Jennifer's had long been promised fully paid health insurance for life. Now, according to office chatter, receipt of this benefit was also in question. Jennifer had no idea what health insurance might cost her down the road if she ended up having to pay the bill as an individual.

Apparently the uncertainties Jennifer was describing led her to new considerations. She had suddenly begun to wonder whether it was time for her to retire. "But the idea of retirement terrifies me," she reported. "What will I do? What if I don't have enough money? What if I get sick?" While the facts being provided to employees were fragmented, Jennifer believed—at this juncture—employees who left sooner would be better off. For instance, those leaving sooner seemed far more likely to walk away with their pension and health insurance benefits intact. Her feeling was, "Those who stayed around? Who knew?"

Though it was not appropriate for me to offer professional comments about her concerns at that time, I was able to listen to Jennifer express her fears.

## How Would You Like to Spend Your Time?

Because Jennifer's concerns continued to incubate, we arranged to sit down together professionally a few months later. By then she had been bombarded with gossip and speculation at work. Apparently, at the time of our meeting, only one "fact" had been revealed by her company: after a certain date, pensions would be calculated using updated life expectancy tables. The updated calculations would result in lower monthly income benefits for most retirees. I also learned that Jennifer's husband had died a couple of years before. So not only did she face retirement planning issues, but she faced them on her own. In the past her husband had ruled the financial roost in their household. He considered his grasp of financial matters far superior to hers.

One of the first questions I asked Jennifer was, "When you think about your money, what thoughts, needs, and feelings come to mind?" Like Lydia, thinking about money scared Jennifer. She had not been taught how to handle money.

Jennifer was not sure she knew enough about managing her finances. True, she had always worked diligently to earn it, but that was different. For example, she was not sure how to put together a retirement-income game-plan. She used to think that was her employer's job. In her mind, she worked hard for an employer who in turn provided her income—not just while she was working, but throughout her retirement as well. Wasn't her pension supposed to take care of her basic needs in retirement?

We started with what she did know. She knew she wanted her money to provide her with financial security. And she knew she wanted to do the right thing with her money. To Jennifer that meant making good decisions. For instance, she confided in me that she hoped she had enough to set aside to be financially independent. She would hate to ever be a burden to her children. I suggested that before taking a closer look at her retirement economics, we start with considering what she might do after retiring. After all, her answers to the "How would you like to spend your time?" question could influence our planning for her finances. This made sense to Jennifer.

I emphasized that everyone's process is different regarding this issue. Some prospective retirees are comfortable only if they have their lifestyle game plan all mapped out before they retire. Others deliberately choose to wait six months to a year before making any decisions about how they want to spend their retirement years. In my experience, retirees who wait to decide how to spend their time want to experience the freedom of living day-to-day spontaneously. This can be especially important to former professionals whose time was tightly prescribed during their working years.

When retirees find themselves ready to add some structure to their days, a myriad of choices are available. For instance, clients who have retired often serve on a board or two, for non-profit or corporate organizations. They add structure to their daily schedule by pursuing lifetime fitness goals: classes at the local gym including yoga or Zumba, regular golfing days, daily walks, or cycling are favorites. Another popular choice is to attend, or even teach, classes for seniors.

In an early conversation with Jennifer I pointed out the need to give some of my clients permission to let go of being "power woman." I reminded her that nowhere is it written that a "doing" lifestyle is superior to a "being" lifestyle. While doing may have been crucial to power women during their working years, it may not be a role they want to carry into retirement. Now, being with family and friends may be the priority. Having the freedom to be caregivers for their grandchildren, for example—especially so their children can pursue their time-demanding career goals—can be a satisfying priority.

## Answering the Question

Before examining Jennifer's response to the question "How would I like to spend my time in retirement?" take a moment to contemplate your own answers to that all-important question. The following bullet points may help stimulate your thinking.

- Retire first. Take a deep breath for six months or so and then chart my retirement journey.
- Chart my steps for post-retirement first. Set the date on which I will retire and then set my retirement game plan into motion.
- Brainstorm answers to this question: "If I could wave a magic wand and do anything I wanted after retiring, what would I do?"
- Serve on corporate or non-profit boards.

- Become a consultant and continue to earn income.
- Focus on fitness. Travel to every state or every continent. Write a book.
- Spend unlimited time with family and friends.

I hope you have now collected some ideas about what makes sense for you. In Jennifer's case, she chose to wait until she had been retired for a while before making any "how I want to spend my time" decisions. Ultimately Jennifer's decision to ease into retirement worked well for her. She maintained her network of connections. About eighteen months after she stopped working, these connections led to consulting work. The consulting work proved lucrative and satisfying, and she felt herself to be the mistress of her own ship in a way she had never been before. Jennifer could now choose when and how much she wanted to work in any given month. She could take vacations whenever she pleased, and her earnings from consulting were a delightful bonus to her retirement income.

## How Have You Prepared to Fund Your Retirement Years?

Jennifer chose to direct her consulting earnings—what she thought of as her bonus earnings—to a specific account she dubbed her inflation hedge account. She was well aware that while working she had looked forward to a raise each year, at least a cost-of-living raise. We had discussed how her current investments might fund annual cost-of-living increases for her in retirement, but she felt more secure knowing she had a separate account just for that purpose. As you can see, Jennifer was a planner.

### Inflation and Income Needs

Now let us take a closer look at her concern about inflation. How does inflation typically affect retirees? Typically inflation has a big impact on how much additional income may be needed year after year, to maintain one's current lifestyle.

Consider these assumptions for a moment. Imagine you are living on $250,000 a year when you prepare to retire at age 66. And let us also assume you have put in place entities that will help you match your $250,000 before retirement income, net of any state or federal income taxes. Yet, questions linger:

- What average rate of inflation should you anticipate?
- Based on that average rate of inflation, by how much will your annual income need to increase?
- How much income will you need ten years hence to have the same buying power as you have on the day you retire?

Well, to stick with our assumptions, you retire at age 66, but only after determining how an average rate of inflation of 3% impacts the income you will likely need ten years into retirement, when you attain age 76. In fact, your calculations result in a need for an annual income of approximately $340,000 net of income taxes by the time you attain age 76.

Yes, to maintain your lifestyle when you attain age 76, you will need $90,000 more in annual income than you needed upon retiring! Another way to think about this is that you will need to increase your income by approximately 35% every ten years, simply to maintain your economic status. And remember, these assumptions do not consider any additions to your expenses, such as choosing to pay for your grandchildren's college educations, facing confiscatory long-term health care expenses, or wanting more income because now you have the time to travel or play golf as often as you wish.

Conversations about inflation are often described in terms of buying power or purchasing power. It is not known how much negative impact inflation will have from one year to the next. But it is known that historically the value of our dollars diminishes over time as illustrated in Figure 10.

# Purchasing Power of U.S. Dollar

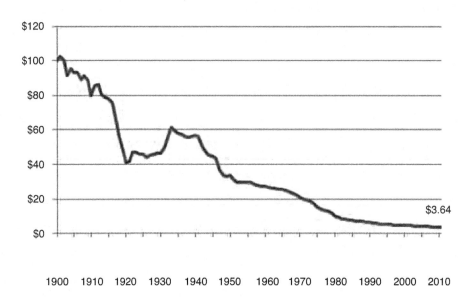

**Figure 10:** Purchasing Power Over Time

*Source:* Observations (ObservationsAndNotes.blogspot.com)

To put it differently, a plan to generate retirement income needs to include a plan to offset the impact of inflation. In fact, as the duration of individual life increases, one also needs to prepare to avoid running out of money.

Returning to the case of Lydia, introduced at the beginning of the chapter, one can infer she had not thought about inflation. She simply assumed anyone with a pension was set for life in terms of retirement income. She seemed not to understand that pensions rarely include a cost-of-living increase component.

Perhaps Lydia was also unaware of a twenty-first century reality. In today's economy many employees are no longer able to count on an employer-guaranteed lifetime pension, whether or not it was originally offered as part of their benefits package. Because corporations and institutions have discovered funding of promised pensions is woefully inadequate, many have chosen to cap existing benefits and switch to other retirement savings choices going forward. The new choices typically require significant employee contributions. They often eliminate employer-guaranteed benefits and transfer the risk of inadequate funding directly to the employees.

The widespread news reporting about the inadequate funding of existing pensions, particularly since 2008, attracted Jennifer's attention and precipitated her decision to retire. Perhaps you, too, are wondering whether a pension you depended upon will in fact be paid.

There is another twenty-first century underfunding concern many Americans face. Baby boomers who waited to have children, perhaps until forty years of age, are becoming retirement age right on the heels of having finished paying college tuition for their offspring. Consequently, parents may have less than a decade between tuition liabilities and the need to fund retirement, the biggest bill of their lives. Moreover, they have little time for intensive saving prior to retirement. Discretionary funds that might have been earmarked for retirement savings are no long available to them, having been directed to pay college expenses instead.

Now that we have taken a look at some retirement funding considerations—the impact of inflation, the uncertainty of pension funding and benefits, and a potential obstacle to saving enough for retirement—it is time to apply these considerations to your own situation. It is time to be specific.

To identify specifics that pertain to your situation, I encourage you to walk through each of the retirement funding to-do's that follow. Thoughtfully make revisions to your own personal planning as you aim for a fully funded retirement lifestyle.

## Retirement Funding To-Do's

- Reconfirm your comfort level with risk, particularly as you move into the distribution phase rather than the contribution phase with respect to your retirement accounts.

- Reconfirm the relationship between your asset allocation decision and your anticipated retirement income distribution rate (safe-max). (See the "Distribution Rate from an Asset Allocation Portfolio" section in Chapter 4.)
- Schedule a meeting with your financial advisor at least six months before your anticipated retirement date.
- Revisit and refine, if needed, your investment planning assumptions. (See Chapter 4, Exercise #2.)
- Schedule meetings with your other related professionals (CPA and estate attorney, for example) as appropriate.
- Revisit and refine, if needed, your Wealth Enhancement Plan. (See Chapter 5, Exercise #2.)
- Revisit and refine, if needed, your Wealth Transfer Plan. (See Chapter 5, Exercise #2.)

Material covered in Chapters 4 and 5 specifically addressed how to construct a strong investment foundation and secure your financial independence. A brief review of these chapters might be useful as you employ the retirement funding to-do's to fine-tune your plans.

## Wealth Protection Strategies

As you concentrate on putting your financial house in order for retirement, considerations about wealth protection are often essential. Wealth protection strategies are the means by which you protect your wealth against potential creditors, litigants, sons-in-law/daughters-in-law or potential ex-spouses. Wealth protection strategies may also be designed to protect you against catastrophic loss.

Even if you implemented wealth protection strategies prior to retirement, revisiting your plans and refining them as needed could be vital to the protection of your style of living in the years ahead. Generally speaking, there are three ways to protect your wealth: correctly titling your assets, using insurance, and executing protective documents such as trusts.

## Titling Your Assets

Protecting your wealth through correctly titling your assets is usually easy to implement and unlikely to cost you anything. Particularly when there is a change in your life circumstances, a review of whether the existing titling of your current assets still offers protection may be imperative. Take the example of Martha, who upon deciding to re-marry wanted to protect her assets from potentially being subject to a future divorce proceeding:

> Prior to her second marriage, Martha decided to title her non-retirement portfolio jointly with her sister. Martha's goal was to reinforce the terms of her prenuptial agreement.

> Her prenuptial agreement stated that none of her pre-marital assets could be subject to any future claims of her husband-to-be. So titling jointly with her sister the portfolio accumulated during her first marriage added a layer of difficulty to deter anyone from trying to lay claim to her premarital accounts at some time in the future.

> Having joint account owners helped protect Martha's wealth.

In Martha's situation, having a joint account owner helped protect her wealth. However, titling an asset jointly with someone else may result in unintended negative consequences. As discussed in Chapter 5, a joint owner of your account must be selected with care. Remember Sandy? She had chosen her daughter as a joint owner, but her daughter squandered most of the funds for her own personal use, a consequence Sandy had not anticipated.

Equally important is the matter of titling a rental property. Perhaps you purchased a dwelling when you were in your early thirties and titled it in your own name. If the property is listed in your name and not held by an LLC or other entity, you run the risk of losing your property as well as unspecified amounts of personal wealth if tenants lodge a personal liability claim against you. Remember, all it takes is one crazy tenant to dissipate your assets in the blink of an eye.

## Insurance for Wealth Protection

A second common way to protect your wealth is through the use of insurance. The world of insurance is complex, and you want to avoid paying for protection beyond what you actually need. Therefore, relying on the professional expertise of a competent insurance agent makes sense. For instance, your insurance agent has probably already recommended umbrella liability coverage for you and your family. This umbrella coverage is cost-effective and offers personal protection against unscrupulous litigants.

Sometimes clients resist my suggestion to purchase umbrella liability coverage because it seems like an extreme measure of protection they are unlikely to need. But consider this true story:

> Liz is an heiress and is married to a successful cardiologist. They retired a few years ago. Considering their affluence, their style of living is not extravagant. But Liz allows herself to enjoy one expensive indulgence, a spectacular horse farm in an area of absolute beauty about ten miles away from the condo in which they live.
>
> Though she rides only occasionally now that she is getting older, Liz still wants her wonderful farm and pastures to be used and enjoyed. So she devised a system whereby riding instructors were able to conduct lessons there as well as board their own horses on the property.
>
> One delightful summer evening an instructor decided to use the pastures for an encounter with her boyfriend, rather than for conducting riding lessons or exercising her horse. Unfortunately, a horse that was grazing in the pasture stepped on them as he wandered. Subsequently the instructor claimed all manner of injuries for which she demanded compensation.

More to the point, the instructor aggressively sued Liz for their injuries and was handsomely rewarded by the court. The fact that the pastures were not intended as a dating venue did not affect the result. In other words, when others perceive an individual to be affluent, they are highly motivated to find an excuse to sue that person for some type of financial gain. Though Liz did not cause the couple's misfortune, she had to pay for their injuries.

## Trusts May Protect Your Wealth

Trust agreements come in many shapes and sizes. When considering a trust, it is important to remember this type of document is a planning tool, not an end in itself. If you are trying to solve a problem, a trust may be the perfect tool to help you accomplish your goals. But just as there is sometimes no need to purchase insurance, there is sometimes no reason to execute a trust.

Trusts are useful when they help individuals protect wealth. Such agreements may provide protection in a variety of ways including:

- Preserving wealth from estate taxes
- Avoiding probate when an estate is settled
- Establishing an income benefit for a spendthrift or debt-ridden adult child
- Transferring an asset or property to children, following lifetime use by a surviving parent
- Preventing assets from being dissipated to pay confiscatory long-term health care expenses

Take a look at Ali's situation, which offers an example of the multiple benefits she derived from executing just one trust. Ali consulted her attorney when she feared her son-in-law might squander her daughter's inheritance should Ali die prematurely. Her son-in-law had proven time and again that he was superb at mishandling money because he viewed money as an impetus to spend. Ali worked with her attorney to establish a generation-skipping trust. This protective trust would generate income for her daughter's lifetime. But neither her daughter nor her son-in-law would have access to the principal. The principal would ultimately go to Ali's grandchildren, whom she adored. This generation-skipping trust also protected Ali's wealth in two additional ways. It preserved the principal in the trust from estate taxes at Ali's death. And when the trust transferred assets to her grandchildren, the probate process was avoided.

Because you cannot control the behavior of others, consideration of wealth protection makes sense. And the more affluent you are, especially as you prepare to retire, the more important it is to consider wealth protection measures. Figure 11 that follows will stimulate your thinking about particular measures that may apply to your wealth protection needs.

As you can see there are many facets to consider as you prepare to retire, from how you will spend time to your financial preparation and protection. Last but not least, there is another component to include in your retirement planning: how to set the stage to retire gracefully.

## How Might You Set the Stage to Retire Gracefully?

For starters, I am reminded of Bessie Smith's quote at the beginning of this chapter: "I've been rich and I've been poor and rich is better." A primary concern regarding how to set the stage to retire gracefully regards the payment of expenses. Of special concern are unknown expenses like those for health care.

Virtually all of us recognize the unpredictability of health care costs. At the same time, we know that as we age our need for care may accelerate. All of us hope not to have health issues. But what if we do? There are numerous methods for addressing the wild card of long-term health care expenses. Which method is best depends on your own situation. Primary options include the purchase of long-term care insurance, choosing to move to a continuing care community, choosing to move to a life care community, or earmarking plenty of money to pay whatever health-related bills come your way.

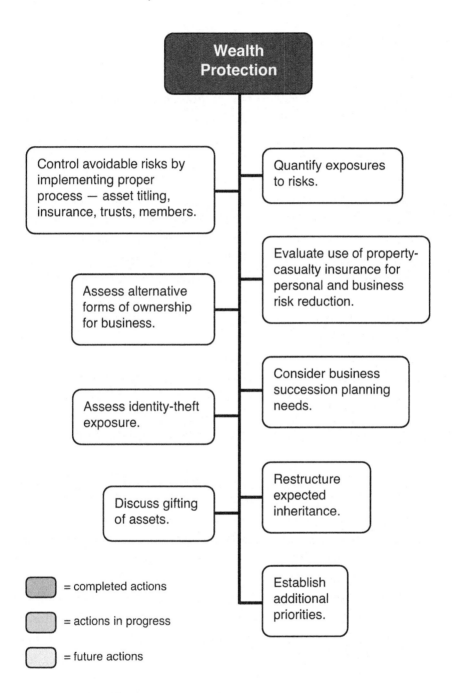

**Figure 11:** Wealth Protection Roadmap

Let us take a moment to understand each of these options. *Long-term care insurance* is an insurance product sold in the United States, United Kingdom, and Canada that provides for the cost of long-term care for a predetermined period. Long-term care insurance covers the cost of care generally not covered by health insurance such as Medicare, or Medicaid. Annual premium payments are typically required to keep the insurance in force.

*Continuing care* and *life care communities* are types of retirement communities. These communities offer to meet a number of elder-care needs within a single residential or community campus. A variety of health care needs are met by providing different living options, including independent living, assisted living, and skilled nursing care. Some communities are designed to provide cottages or apartments for independent living. For those with assisted-living needs, apartments or bed-sitting rooms are offered. Private or semi-private rooms are offered to residents needing skilled nursing care.

Continuing care communities are typically priced on a "pay for what you need" basis. In other words, if you live independently and your needs are few, your monthly costs are assessed from the low end of the pricing scale. On the other hand, if you need skilled nursing care, your monthly costs will be assessed from the high end of the scale. More services are more expensive.

The life care community option is typically priced differently. It utilizes a level pay-as-you-go pricing model. In other words, upon moving into the community, a level base monthly fee is charged to all owners regardless of the type of care needed. This policy can be helpful for planning purposes because unlike the continuing care model, as your need for care increases, your costs do not increase accordingly.

How do these expenses typically get paid? Figure 12 following offers perspective, using the need for assisted living as an example. The illustration indicates what percentage of people rely on insurance to foot the bill. Only 2% of those needing assisted living count on insurance to cover the cost. 75% of those needing assisted living, however, rely on their family to pay the bill.

It is important to note a couple of things. First of all, if settling into a

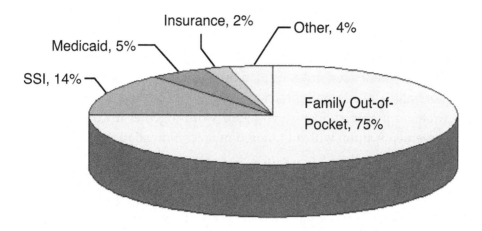

**Figure 12:** Assisted Living: Who Pays?

continuing care or life care community appeals to you, it is important to move before you become ill or experience health-related limitations. Health problems can make you ineligible to move into the community. Second, unless you have enough money set aside so you need not ask the price, you want to consider moving while you have a choice regarding selection of a community with your preferred pricing structure. Otherwise, if you wait until you must move, availability could be limited. Remember, communities with more favorable pricing schedules often have long waiting lists for entry.

## Balancing Act Implications

Delineating a retirement plan to enable you to transition with grace into that stage of your life begins with envisioning the style of living you prefer. Having identified your preferences, the next step is to prepare for the funding you will need so you are not haunted by concerns about running out of money. After all, the bill for your retirement will likely be substantial. Finally, implementing wealth protection strategies may help you avoid feelings of fear like those Lydia expressed earlier in the chapter, as well as help ensure you will not be blindsided someday by catastrophic costs such as those triggered by potential health care needs.

Because, as previously stated, you may have only one chance to get your retirement economics right, a brief examination of the balancing act of values, needs, and interests Kathryn faced when delineating her retirement plan may inspire you. Our work together uncovered three key elements, upon which I tailored my recommendations:

1. As a widowed mom with both elderly parents still living, Kathryn chose to think first about how to fund her retirement. She valued feeling financially secure before offering aid to her children and parents.

2. Second, she made certain she could contribute to the expense of the college educations her two children needed—with help from their earnings, too.

3. Third, she was interested in assisting her parents when they needed to move to a life care community. Her father had been showing signs of Alzheimer's and her mother wanted to live close to him, no matter what level of care he might someday need.

Kathryn's willingness to prepare thoughtfully resulted in a strong sense of security as she transitioned with grace into retirement. She also reported feeling a sense of financial independence knowing her family's needs had been addressed, too. Kathryn shared, "I am thrilled to be retired and no longer worrying."

Take the time needed to complete the following exercises, and you may be better prepared to have a retirement experience similar to the one Kathryn achieved.

### Exercise #1: Your Retirement Preferences

If you haven't already, take a moment to answer two questions that were posed earlier. If you answered them before, revisit each and add details to your answers. Remember that the more detailed your considerations, the more likely you are to fulfill your values and preferences.

1. When I think about my money, what thoughts, needs, and feelings come to mind?
2. If I could wave a magic wand and do anything I wanted after retiring, what would I do?

Create a YouTube video or collage of photographs to illustrate your answers. Fashioning an image of what you want to achieve or enjoy helps crystallize your thinking.

### *Exercise #2: Wealth Protection Concerns*

Now that you spent time ascertaining your retirement values and preferences, it is time to address the need for protection. A good starting place is to name three wealth protection risks you will likely face in retirement. Examples include:

1. Personal liability due to a vacation property you own
2. Professional liability due to your work as a consultant after you retire
3. Funding liabilities resulting from long-term care costs in your later years

After you identify your personal risks, consult with your insurance agent for  recommendations on how to reduce them. For example, common risk-reduction strategies for retirees include:

- Updating of property and casualty coverage as circumstances change, including umbrella liability coverage
- Considering the purchase of professional insurance if you offer consulting services after retiring
- Considering the purchase of long-term care insurance

**Part II: Protect Your Lifestyle Now and into Retirement** introduced technical material and strategies designed to help you and your family be prepared to experience financial security and independence today and into the future. While we may be able to map out our journey using neatly designed diagrams, we know that life rarely unfolds exactly as expected. **Part III: Leave Fear Behind** begins by addressing what to do when confronted by the unexpected.

# Leave Fear Behind

Most women experience fear when they think about money. They routinely fear they are not making the correct financial decisions and that others make better financial decisions than they do. The fear of becoming destitute may lurk in the back of their minds. Take, for example, a comment made by Katie Couric on *The Today Show* in the early 1990s. During casual conversation on the show one morning, she mentioned that her greatest fear in life was one day becoming a bag lady. Her comment left a strong impression because it seemed absurd. After all, she was among the highest paid women in the country.

I have since learned that high wages do not necessarily translate into financial confidence. Nor do large portfolios and financial acuity. While more than 40 percent of American women indicate they are financially literate, fewer than 20 percent report a sense of financial confidence. Nevertheless, I believe financial literacy and financial confidence can become second nature to women, especially if they engage in a holistic process to fulfill their wealth management needs.

The holistic wealth management approach presented in Chapter 5 recognizes the balancing act required for women as they aim to make the right decisions with their money. Balancing values, needs, and interests with an understanding of the fundamentals of money management and with strategic flexibility in the face of change and uncertainty is a tall order. But by using a holistic system, balance is possible. And remember that decisions require monitoring and fine-tuning from time to time, particularly in times of crisis and change. In Chapter 7 that follows, we will consider how you can help yourself prepare for the unexpected, specifically how to manage when confronted by the crisis of a spouse's death or divorce.

As we learned earlier, women have a strong commitment to giving back to their communities. They choose to do so through volunteerism and a variety of forms of charitable giving. Chapter 8 encourages readers to design a personal strategy for a lifetime of giving.

Lastly, Chapter 9 discusses the capacity of women to pursue leadership roles and some of the benefits resulting from their commitment and pursuits.

# CHAPTER 7

# Prepare for the Unexpected

*"In the long run, you make your own luck—*
*good, bad, or indifferent."*

—Loretta Lynn

Back in the 1980s I loved watching the television series, *The A-Team*. My zest for this show puzzled me because I rarely found television interesting. But I loved viewing the episodes, waiting for the denouement when the leader of the team, Hannibal, would say, "I love it when a plan comes together." The A-Team's "plan" always included resolving a crisis at hand. The need to resolve a crisis was posited in the first few minutes of the show; then obstacles would occur, making resolution seem impossible. Predictable? You bet. But somehow, some way, the A-Team would relentlessly pursue their desired outcome(s). They would face or bypass each obstacle along the way as they moved onward to the desired resolution. Though their pathway to success might require changing directions more than once, with their eyes on the target they would ultimately prevail. The essence of their plan would inevitably come together.

When a crisis occurs in your life, you will not be able to call the A-Team to rescue you. But as unexpected events of lesser or greater magnitude are bound to occur, you need to be ready to respond effectively.

To help you prepare for the unexpected, this chapter offers a response framework.

Three practical concepts are employed—control, equanimity, and actuation—selected for their usefulness in eliminating fear and purposefully sidestepping obstacles. Descriptions of the experience of Pauline and Julie are offered to illustrate how this response framework actually functions.

## The Unexpected: Loss of Your Spouse

One of two major life crises confronts the majority of women at least once during their lives: loss of a spouse and/or divorce. Why do I suggest the majority of us will face one or the other? Recent statistics indicate that 80 percent of American men die while married. On the other hand, 80 percent of American women die alone.[5]

Regarding divorce, statistics have indicated for decades that half of all Americans are divorced at least once. Whether a spouse dies or a marriage dissolves, most women will one day be on their own.[6] That is, some portion of their later years will be lived solo. The emotional impact of these statistics is staggering. Consider for a moment adding financial concerns to the mix. Paralyzing fear can result.

One of the most compelling fears following a spouse's death is, "Will I (my family) be okay financially?" And this concern may be just as intense whether your spouse was ill for a period of time preceding his death or his death was sudden. I experienced this fear when my husband died in 2008, even though I was a financial advisor.

---

[5]SmallSteps for Big Change Blog, "You'll Probably Die Alone." Posted March 10, 2010, https://smallstepsforbigchange.wordpress.com/2010/03/10/youll-probably-die-alone

[5]Statistics from the McKinley Irvin Family Law Blog, "32 Shocking Divorce Statistics." October 2012, https://www.mckinleyirvin.com/Family-Law-Blog/2012/October/32-Shocking-Divorce-Statistics.aspx

Fear often springs from a variety of financial unknowns following the death of a spouse. Such unknowns include: "Is there debt? How will I take care of our children? Am I the survivor beneficiary on his pension? How in the world will I generate enough income going forward? Will I be able to continue the lifestyle we enjoyed when he was living?"

Many women are left with these unknowns because even today, often the man has taken care of most financial matters for the family. Perhaps you balanced the checkbook or figured out how much you saved when making purchases of items on sale. But the "real" financial matters were assumed by him.

No wonder when women become widows or divorcees, they feel terrified. They are faced with the need to take control of their financial lives for the first time ever.

## Control

My client Pauline found herself suddenly single about eight years ago. Her husband died unexpectedly at the age of fifty-three. In our first conversation following his death, Pauline shared with me thoughts that continued to replay in her mind. "This couldn't have happened. He was okay. Other women become widows. Other women whose husbands are old."

As you have probably been able to discern, an underlying theme in the thoughts Pauline shared is control. She desperately wanted to control the situation in which she found herself. She wanted to replay the scene in order to achieve a different outcome. Not surprisingly, she wanted to make this life-changing event disappear. I mention this as an observation only, free of any judgment.

As you know from your own experiences with death, a period of shock follows. Shock is part of the grieving process. And I believe some degree of denial is normal, too. Denial may be crucial as the survivor slowly begins to recognize the enormity of the life changes ushered in by death, life changes the survivor did not choose. Nothing will ever be the same. You can replay the scene but you cannot reverse the result. Nevertheless, you can help yourself by focusing on the things you can control. This common-sense wisdom has been memorialized in the first four lines of The Serenity Prayer:

**The Serenity Prayer**

*God grant me the serenity*
*To accept the things I cannot change;*
*Courage to change the things I can;*
*And wisdom to know the difference.*

Pauline did not want to be miserable. So she willingly mustered the courage to focus on what she could control. When we first talked together following the death of her husband, Pauline revealed her perspective. She said the death of her husband was "the hardest smack life ever dished out to me." She concluded the lessons she needed to learn from this event must be big and emphasized, "I truly want to be open to learning them."

Feeling that her husband's death presented her with opportunities to learn enabled Pauline to recognize she had control in determining how to respond. As we talked I encouraged her to write down three important things she could control. She wrote:

- Remind my two children that while one parent has passed, they still have a parent: me.
- Keep in the forefront of my mind that I am not alone. I have my family and wonderful friends—lots of people who love me.
- Continue making a contribution in the work that I do.
  I want to be engaged in life, just as I was when my husband was living.

Pauline's list revealed she was at an advanced stage in thinking about her circumstances. For others, depending on the degree of shock they experience, recalibrating to feel a sense of control may require smaller steps. For example, shock often affects people physically. Therefore, three smaller steps on your list might be:

- Eat three nutritious meals each day.
- Take a walk (preferably outside) every morning.

- Find ways to relax prior to bedtime so you can sleep well.

You get the idea. You can control taking care of yourself. And taking care of yourself—by now you know what works best for you—can provide a basis for healing as you move into a new phase of life without a beloved spouse.

## The Unexpected: A Divorce Proceeding

Recent statistics suggest that poverty levels escalate for unmarried American women who attain the age of 65 and older, often because they divorce.[7] Sometimes he walks out the door but more often than not she walks, maybe after a marriage of twenty years or longer. This alarming statistic citing poverty levels for older women is exacerbated by our longer life expectancy. Women are likely to live about five years longer than men. Like me, I am certain you do not want to fall into the undesirable statistical group of older women living in poverty. Therefore you need to get prepared, preferably when you are younger and all is well.

Julie became an advocate for such preparedness after she was blindsided by an unexpected divorce proceeding. Her husband walked out the door after twenty-one years of marriage, and like so many wives, she was caught totally unaware of her finances. Her husband had always insisted on managing their family's economic life.

For example, her husband had always encouraged Julie to work only part-time even though Julie was inclined to work full-time. Their two children were nearly launched and did not need much of her attention anymore. But because she wished to respect her husband's preferences, she did not pursue the matter of full-time work.

To complicate the situation, Julie's husband walked out at the beginning of 2009 at the height of the recession. The job market was in a slump and there were few opportunities for Julie to find full-time employment with a competitive salary.

Although Julie's crisis was different from Pauline's, her need for

---

[7]*CNN Money* "Why Many Retired Women Live In Poverty."
http://money.cnn.com/2014/05/13/retirement/retirement-women

healing was just as great. Her life had taken a drastic turn and matters were beyond her control. Taking charge of what she could control, however, enabled her to recover.

Julie's first task was to create a budget. As she emphasized to me, "I won't feel safe until I know where the money is. And I won't feel safe until I know how much income I need each month. And I need to know where the money is coming from for the periodic larger bills and our annual vacation. He may have left me, but my kids and I are still a family and we are still going to vacation together every summer. I need to know I can afford that."

## Budgeting

Let us pause Julie's story for a moment and dive a bit deeper into the activity of budgeting. Whether you are blindsided like Julie because your husband takes off or *you* choose to uncouple, you need to know where you stand regarding your income and expenses. This understanding is fundamental to landing on your feet post-divorce. Assuming you do not have a detailed budget (few of us do), it may be because budgeting often triggers an emotional reaction.

For example, my mother used her budgeting endeavors as a report card. But her grades always ended up below average. Her arithmetic was always A+ but her commitment to upholding her self-imposed budget numbers was poor. Consequently, her budgeting failures led to self-criticism and guilt.

Because mapping out a budget is fundamental to your ability to take control of your life post-divorce, set aside your emotions and feelings about the past and forge ahead. I encourage you to think of creating this budget as an opportunity to look straight into the present. If necessary, remind yourself that budget numbers are not about the past. They are about the here and now and the foreseeable future.

To make this process more palatable, I suggest you call the spreadsheet you will make a spending plan rather than a budget; after all, the intention of the work is to identify the amount of money you have to spend. When you have identified the sum you have to spend, then you allocate from that amount the precise number of dollars you *must have* to meet your needs. After allocating for your needs, you can begin to consider the things you *want*.

### Spending Plan Step 1: Start with Your Income

Gather together the last two or three years of income tax returns. Take a look at all the sources of income that flow into the household. Next, logon to **Balancingactbook.com**, click on **Resources**, and download your Chapter 7 *Spending Plan* worksheet. Transfer your individual income numbers from your tax returns onto your Spending Plan worksheet.

Spending Plan Income categories include:

| INCOME | MONTHLY | ANNUALLY |
|---|---|---|
| **Work** | | |
| Salary | $ _____ | $ _____ |
| Tips | $ _____ | $ _____ |
| | | |
| **Other** | | |
| Alimony | $ _____ | $ _____ |
| Bonus | $ _____ | $ _____ |
| Child Support | $ _____ | $ _____ |
| Dividends/Interest | $ _____ | $ _____ |
| Pension | $ _____ | $ _____ |
| Retirement Distributions | $ _____ | $ _____ |
| Social Security | $ _____ | $ _____ |
| | $ _____ | $ _____ |
| | $ _____ | $ _____ |

While married, you probably filed income taxes jointly with your spouse. Going forward, this will no longer be the case. If you cannot yet identify your individual income, leave the income entries blank until your anticipated individual income amounts and/or sources are confirmed.

### *Step 2: Think About Your Expenses*

Now the real work begins. (You can finish reading this chapter first if that is better for you. Just don't lose momentum.) Take a look at every category on the Chapter 7 *Spending Plan* worksheet you downloaded from the **Resources** tab of **Balancingactbook.com**). Fill in each blank that pertains to your own lifestyle. Make these entries either on a monthly or an annual basis, whatever seems more user-friendly.

Remember, you cannot simply identify the monthly expenses you had while married and divide them down the middle. Going forward, when you and your ex-spouse live in separate households, each home will incur its own set of expenses. This means it will in all likelihood cost more to live post-divorce than when you were married and living under one roof.

Your *Spending Plan* worksheet will illustrate at a glance what it will cost you to live. The expenses framework will tell you how much you will need at a minimum per month to maintain your current style of living after divorce. And remember, taking the time to get the numbers right may enhance your well-being for years to come.

After completing your spending plan, you will probably be ready to tackle other aspects of your divorce negotiation. If you discovered an income shortfall now that two households require funding, it is time to sharpen your pencil.

Sharpening your pencil entails evaluating each expense and trimming or eliminating any expense that is not essential. Generally speaking, you do not want to spend down retirement savings for current income, because there may not be time to replace those funds before you are ready to retire.

If you do A+ arithmetic like my mother and stick to your numbers, you may be pleasantly surprised. Julie certainly was. Focusing on her spending plan gave Julie a starting place for taking charge of her independence.

To reiterate, unexpected events like losing your spouse or confronting a divorce are difficult emotionally. However, the healing process begins when you take small steps in the direction of assuming command of what you can control.

Regardless of the nature of the catastrophic event, nurturing yourself is essential. Included in the act of self-nurturing is taking care of your financial well-being. Therefore, possessing a fundamental understanding of your income and expenses is a vital step on the pathway of healing.

Pauline and Julie began to gradually assume control of their new lives despite the catastrophic event with which each was confronted. They slowly moved past their initial states of shock to the next phase, where they began to strive for equanimity in their lives.

## Equanimity

Striving for equanimity, defined as evenness of mind especially under stress (Merriam-Webster.com), is instrumental to healing. Just speaking the word equanimity aloud conjures up the sense of a blanket of calm descending to envelope us. Two characteristics of this emotional state are composure and self-possession. Ah . . . mental relaxation. I believe as you recover from the shock of something as life-changing as the death of your spouse or divorce, and then initially reestablish a sense of control over your life, a natural second step on your pathway of healing is to focus on the experience of equanimity.

But women tend to be unnecessarily self-critical, so equanimity can seem elusive. For example, when conducting interviews with dozens of women for this book, the following themes emerged from the majority of the women interviewed:

1. "I am always pressed for time."
2. "No matter what, I can never get enough done."

3. "I was never taught how to handle money."

4. "I don't know enough about managing my finances."

These themes were common despite the fact that only half of the women interviewed had ever been confronted by the shock of the unexpected death of a spouse or divorce.

Pauline struggled with some of the same concerns identified in the interviews. For instance, being pressed for time and getting enough done were high on her list of self-criticisms. In her mind, she needed to be on high alert for what other people might need because a big part of her identity involved taking care of others first. In the past, she had rarely thought of herself until everyone else's needs were satisfied. Pauline had never questioned those inclinations until one day, about ten months after her husband's death, she caught herself saying yes to something she did not wish to do. She suddenly realized she had enough going on in her life at the moment and did not want to make another commitment.

"What a wake-up call," she recollected. "You know, after my husband died, I quickly took on the habit of saying yes to just about everything. I wanted to be super busy and I didn't want to spend the evening alone. At first I enjoyed saying yes to everyone, friends and family. It made me feel needed again. But all of a sudden I found myself wanting to put my foot on the brake. People were starting to take advantage of me. Even my family was."

As our discussions unfolded, Pauline clearly stated her desire to attend to her individual needs in the interest of experiencing equanimity. While immediately following the death of her husband she had been preoccupied with struggling to gain some control in her life and with accepting her new situation, she now felt ready to recalibrate. Pauline could see that going forward, her sense of equanimity depended on learning to say yes to herself and no to endless requests, including family favors.

Conversely, Julie's journey of achieving equanimity was different from Pauline's. Hers had a decidedly financial flavor. Julie felt she had to stand firm and keep saying *no* to financial requests. She was bombarded with family requests to pay for goods and services, things that were not part of her carefully formulated spending plan. Because she had not learned how to handle money in the past, creating her spending plan had special significance, which helped her regain a sense of control and confidence. Meanwhile, her divorcing husband's behavior seemed to purposefully undermine the stability and confidence she had achieved. For example, he encouraged their children to ask her for the extra things they wanted so he would not have to pay for them. He made negative comments to them about Julie's spending: "She's bleeding me dry. I won't have anything left when she gets done with me." He wanted the children to believe Julie was not pulling her weight economically and he was stuck paying too many bills.

You can imagine the emotions his behavior aroused. But Julie ignored his tactics and steadfastly protected her spending plan. She achieved stability as a consequence. For Julie, financial security was a crucial component of a balanced lifestyle. Feeling secure in her financial life meant financial independence was still within reach despite the curveball life had thrown her. Julie vowed to continue learning what she needed to know about managing her finances in order to ensure attainment of financial security and independence.

Generally speaking, Pauline discovered it was necessary to value her own needs as highly as those of her family and friends, while Julie remained firm in saying no to expenses not covered by her spending plan. In different ways, each woman embraced the responsibility to make choices aimed at introducing balance into their lives. Remarkably, neither woman permitted herself to become an emotional hostage to the expectations of others.

## Actuation

Taking steps to regain control and rebuild equanimity requires willingness to move forward rather than experiencing life through a rearview mirror lens. Actuation, that is propelling oneself forward, can be hard because it demands that we let go. And it is comfortable to focus on the known joys of the past rather than stepping out into the unknowns to come. But exercising a tendency to hold on and ruminate is unlikely to help anyone's journey to healing. If you notice yourself dwelling on the past, I encourage you not to succumb. Instead, take some small action— immediately when possible—to reinforce a sense of control as well as forward momentum in your life. Actuation through the completion of these small actions becomes a form of claiming ownership of the new life you are creating.

Pauline practiced a tangible form of claiming ownership. While her husband was still alive, their dining room reflected his distinctive decorative preferences. But Pauline had never really cared for his decorative style, so she gave herself permission to redecorate her dining room. At first it was jarring to think of it as "her" dining room rather than "our" dining room. She wasn't at all sure she wanted to let go of what he had liked because that would sever their connection even more. But moving forward was not negotiable. With the help of shouting some of her favorite expletives, she reminded herself that instituting changes and stepping into the future required practice. So practice she did. Her completely redecorated dining room now serves as tangible proof of her journey of healing.

Julie's journey of claiming ownership was helped immeasurably by incorporating music in her life. She has a good friend, a practicing psychologist, who waited a few months after Julie's separation before mentioning the healing power of music, especially singing. At first Julie resisted. How was she going to enjoy singing all those tunes she had once enjoyed? They were all about love, right? Julie knew her friend meant well, but really! Nevertheless the idea appealed to her and eventually she gave it a try. The music and lyrics of Stephen Sondheim were some of Julie's favorites. One day when she faced a long drive in the car, she pulled out a Bernadette Peters concert CD. She had forgotten that the last cut on the disc was Sondheim's "Move On." While "Move On" is essentially a love song, the opening lyrics inspired Julie.

**Move On**
Lyrics by Stephen Sondheim

*Stop worrying where you're going — move on.*
*If you can know where you're going, you've gone.*
*Just keep moving on.*

*I chose, and my world was shaken — so what?*
*The choice may have been mistaken, the choosing was not.*
*You have to move on.*

*Move on.*

Julie soon realized her friend was right. While some tears may have flowed while she was singing in her car, something else was happening, too: a renewed feeling of hope. Her sense of hope was renewed every time she sang. Sometime later Julie said, "I am seeing that hope is fundamental to actuation, fundamental to claiming ownership of my new life."

## Balancing Act Implications

Most women will experience the loss of a spouse or face divorce at some point in their lives. No two of us will respond to the crisis in exactly the same way, but the need to heal will be a common thread we all share. The journey of healing after an unexpected life-changing event is personal and your process will be unique. Perhaps, you will be able to take heart from the experiences of Pauline and Julie. Their responses revealed the healing benefits of choice. Both women benefitted from choosing to gain control and establish equanimity. Each woman eventually rekindled hope and gave herself permission to step forward and make changes.

The Balancing Act implications with respect to your wealth planning following a crisis are potentially great. You may discover the need to revisit some or all of your former planning documents. You are the sole decision-maker now. Your financial advisor, serving in the role of coach, may be instrumental in this part of your journey of healing. Being able to turn to an objective, trusted advisor as a sounding board can provide just the anchor you require as you reevaluate your financial strategy in light of your changed circumstances.

Should you engage in a new primary relationship, consider drafting a legal agreement called a prenuptial agreement. It is an agreement made by a couple, typically before they marry, and is drafted and executed by an attorney. The agreement confirms ownership of the couple's respective assets. Such an agreement is usually implemented out of concern that the marriage might someday end. However, particularly with second relationships and blended families in the mix, such an agreement can help delineate what belongs to whom and what will belong to whom should a death occur.

At the beginning of this chapter I raised a universal fear: "Will I be okay financially?" Now let us turn to a couple of exercises that may help you elude that fear and always answer that question with a resounding, "Yes, I will be okay!"

### Exercise #1: Spending Plan Worksheet

If you have not already done so, set aside some quiet time for supplying the data to complete your *Spending Plan* worksheet. As mentioned previously, logon to **Balancingactbook.com**, click on **Resources**, and download your Chapter 7 *Spending Plan* worksheet. Although this is not an easy task, completing it can save you heartache because you will finally know where you stand financially—an important step in taking charge of your personal finances.

### Exercise #2: Revise Your Planning

If you have been confronted by an unexpected occurrence, turn back to the *Balancing Act Implications* and the *Exercises* sections of the previous chapters. Re-consider the results of the exercises and the planning you completed for these six chapters. The following roadmap (Figure 13) is

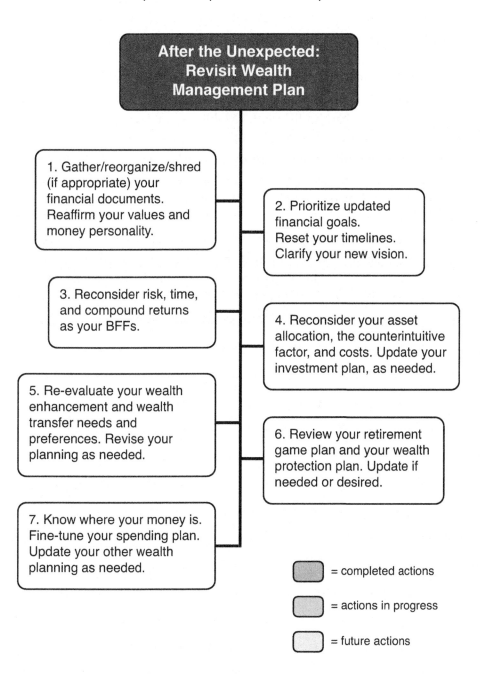

**Figure 13:** After the Unexpected Roadmap

a chapter-by-chapter guide to prompt your thinking about revisions you might need to make. Update your original documents as appropriate.

As this chapter closes you may be interpreting our opening Loretta Lynn sentiment a bit more strategically: "In the long run you make your own luck—good, bad, indifferent." Making your own good luck sometimes requires turning lemons into lemonade. Said another way, influencing your luck can require confronting and analyzing your emotions as well as completing concrete planning tasks. The emotional work is often the most difficult, but I believe you will discover the final outcome is worth the effort.

Women have a strong commitment to knowing what they can do with their money. A strong interest shared by many women regarding what they can do is to develop opportunities to give back to the greater community. Chapter 8, "What to Do if You Choose to Give Back," delves into a variety of ways to fulfill your charitable interests.

CHAPTER 8

# Fulfill Your Charitable Aspirations

*"You have everything you need right now to be an
extraordinary philanthropist."*

—Laura Arrillaga-Andreessen

The previous chapter required emotional work that was perhaps difficult and painful. In this chapter we are going to continue considering
emotional issues, but we are switching gears to contemplate how to
organize charitable giving. I can almost promise this discussion about
gift giving will involve feel-good emotions only. In fact, medical
research has shown that the emotions you feel when you grant or
bestow gifts are good indeed.[8] Medical tests have indicated that giving
of your time, your talents, or your money stimulates a part of the brain
that results in the same gratification as when you eat food or have sex.

Not only will fulfilling your charitable aspirations feel good, a by-
product of choosing to give is the enhancement of your sense of confidence in three powerful ways:

1. You are taking action, and action builds confidence.

2. You are affirming gratitude, and gratitude is a powerful confidence builder.

[8]Arrillaga-Andreessen, Laura. *Giving 2.0: Transform Your Giving and Our World*. New
York: Jossey-Bass, 2011.

3. You are aligning your money with your values, and it is empowering to know your money is serving personally important purposes.

Clearly, contributing to charitable causes is a win-win. But many women are not sure how to put their aspirations into practice, and financial advisors not ascribing to a holistic wealth management approach are unlikely to pursue this conversation with their clients. Therefore, while earlier chapters offered guidance about managing your wealth and protecting your style of living, this chapter offers tangible guidance designed to help you explore your philanthropic aspirations.

A philanthropist is one who gives passion, compassion, financial gifts, or knowledge. In light of these attributes, this chapter will emphasize:

- Giving time and energy
- Giving money
- Enhancing the culture of giving in your community

According to philanthropist Laura Arrillaga-Andreessen, "You have everything you need right now to be an extraordinary philanthropist." By the end of this chapter I hope you will feel empowered to take action and will experience enhanced personal confidence—one of the many positive consequences of choosing to give.

## Giving Time and Energy

Giving time and energy can be an effective stimulus to your philanthropic aspirations. Consider what you are passionate about and what needs exist in your local community. Of course you can achieve your philanthropic aspirations by giving time and energy beyond your immediate community. But I guarantee you will discover some needs close to home that will benefit from your compassion and expertise. For example, Anna discovered she could satisfy her philanthropic aspirations within a ten-mile radius of her home. That suited her because she wanted to spend her time teaching, not commuting.

When her two college-aged children left the nest, Anna felt ready for a substantial volunteering endeavor. Due to her training as an elementary school teacher, she was attracted to becoming an adult literacy volunteer. For more than three decades now, Anna has served as a literacy volunteer in her community. She has worked with numerous waves of immigrants. Without leaving her hometown, she traveled the world and experienced multiple cultures. Anna's students were usually assigned to her shortly after they arrived on American soil. She has taught English to Vietnamese, Korean, Russian, Iraqi, Serbian, and Croatian immigrants—to name a few. Many of her students knew few words of English when they landed in her classroom. She has reported countless heart-wrenching stories revealing their sense of inadequacy as they faced life in a country where they could not communicate.

It was Anna's job to teach her students rudimentary English, spoken and written, but Anna taught them so much more. She was the face of America to her immigrant students. She offered them the hope of acclimating to and communicating in a new world, a world forced on them because life in their home countries had become untenable. Anna's tireless efforts were recognized by the state in which she lives when she was awarded her state's Literacy Volunteer of the Year award in 2002.

## Philanthropy and the Next Generation

Not surprisingly, parents who volunteer their time become role models leading their children and grandchildren to seek relevant opportunities for community service. These gifts of community service not only shape the values of the next generation but can provide young people with extracurricular activities college admissions boards like to see. Founding executive director of Tulane University's Center for Public Service (CPS) Vincent Illustre highlighted this paradigm when he said, "We are seeing more and more high schools and middle school require service hours. We're looking beyond that, for stellar community service activities."[9]

---

[9]NobleHour blog. "How Volunteering and Service Can Help with College Admissions," Dolly Duplantier. November 6, 2013 @ 9 AM.

Actually, Anna's experience provides a good example of what universities are looking for. She followed her passion for teaching when choosing her volunteering endeavor and supported it with her training and expertise. Universities want proof that admission candidates have engaged in a sustained community service activity or two, and they want proof that the activity was selected on the basis of the student's passion and commitment. "Once and done" or short-term efforts are not considered remarkable. To evaluate the commitment to service of prospective students, a university admissions office often seeks and evaluates answers to questions such as:

- How does this student frame her giving-back activities?
- What is her rhyme and reason for this particular endeavor?
- What made her undertake this particular project?

Tulane University is nationally known for its leadership in focusing on personal and public service as core elements of a twenty-first-century education. They offer some specific suggestions for your high school child or grandchild, which include:

- Explore a variety of volunteering interests during freshman and sophomore years of high school.
- Select one or maybe two topics or issues of interest by the beginning of your junior year in high school. Research organizations that support these interests.
- Now take the interest to the next step. Delve deeper. Enthusiastically pursue community engagement with the issue selected.

Like Tulane University, a growing number of universities are focusing on public service as a core element of higher education. For that reason, a substantive commitment to community service may even help position your child or grandchild to be awarded scholarship assistance.

## Giving Money

Just as we teach young children to share, most of us adults want to share, too. And that includes our financial resources, not simply our time. In fact, America tends to be a generous nation. About 95 percent of us contribute money annually to causes for which we care deeply. Our national desire to give back to the community was recently cited as a chief motivation for our gifts.

Similarly, the concept of giving money for the benefit of others has been present across the globe for centuries. For instance, it is fundamental to many religious teachings. In fact, a number of religions expect their faithful to tithe. Often the tithing contribution identified in religious teachings is 10 percent of what you earn. Whether you choose to tithe or to give whatever you believe you can afford, many of us women would prefer to give more. But we fear we might run short of money if we are charitable. Or we rationalize that our gifts won't make that much difference anyway, especially if we compare them to sizable foundational gifts like those of Bill and Melinda Gates or Warren Buffett.

About eight years ago, Stella, my colleague, decided she wanted to pursue serving on a board. To that end, she started a dialogue with the leadership team of a small arts organization in her local community. She chose the organization because she loved art and was interested in giving back to the arts, an arena that is often overlooked by donors. Now, eight years later, her contribution of time, energy, and money has transformed the giving culture of the organization, and her quiet efforts have become a potent illustration of return on investment.

Stella spent the first few years getting to know the organization by serving on its board. Next she took advantage of an opportunity to help the arts group plan in detail their upcoming annual budget. For a number of years the organization had become accustomed to the concept of living *beyond* their means. This practice led them to follow the strategy of "buy now, pay later," as illustrated by the large bills they incurred for their building. Rather than planning ahead for inevitable repairs and periodic replacement of things such as the HVAC system, they waited for a crisis to occur and then tapped into their line of credit to pay the unexpected bill. Naturally, this practice increased their costs due to the monthly principal and interest payments that would continue for years into the future while they slowly repaid the credit line.

Stella urged the board to reverse their thinking. She encouraged them to consider the economic impact they would derive from living *within* their means. Making this strategic change of thinking was not easy. For instance, the means or income of the board fluctuated annually according to gifts and grants received, which were influenced by the economy. Understandably, planning for unpredictable large expenses can seem to be an untenable goal when annual revenues are uncertain. In addition, implementation of the concept of living within one's means would result in board members receiving a challenge. They would be expected to contribute an increased amount of financial support—that is, to pay higher annual dues.

No one could remember the last time annual dues were recalibrated. Now, with unanimous board approval, a schedule of increases was adopted for a period of three years. The group believed that the increased board dues would be sufficient to cover a portion of the organization's annual operating expenses in order to avoid being hurt by income short-falls during economic times when revenues were somewhat diminished. Moreover, Stella advanced three benefits of this strategy:

1. With a portion of basic operating expenses covered, there would not be a need to tap into a line of credit for funding; this would save the organization quite a bit of money in the years ahead.

2. When applying for grants they were more likely to be awarded funding if their budget was in balance and not debt-dependent. Donors prefer giving to a successful organization, and a balanced budget is a key indicator of success.

3. General fund-raising efforts were more likely to be successful because a larger proportion of money raised would go directly to programs. And most individual funders prefer to help people rather than to help the organization keep the lights on.

Generally speaking, Stella was pleased that her suggestions were valued and adopted. Furthermore, because she aspired to make a financial gift to a cause that was personally important, she decided now was the time. After discussing with the organization's leadership team what she had in mind, Stella gifted $25,000 to institute a stability fund for the organization. Her gift provided the seed money for a fund to generate earnings that could be tapped for extraordinary expenses, thus helping end the organization's cycle of living beyond their means. In the meantime, the board achieved a balanced budget and secured substantial board support in the form of increased dues.

Now that the leadership team was energized by their accomplishments, they felt ready to approach a local foundation with a request for a gift of $50,000. The foundation countered with a qualified yes. They agreed to honor the request if the board would match Stella's gift dollar-for-dollar. In other words, the foundation would match whatever amount the board was willing to commit to the organization.

It is easy to see why Stella expressed pleasure as she told me her story. Her gift of $25,000 to institute the stability fund was quickly matched by contributions from individual board members totaling more than an additional $25,000. With a total of over $50,000 in the stability fund, the organization returned to the foundation to seek a matching sum of $50,000. Accordingly, the request was granted. To put it another way, within six months, Stella's $25,000 gift grew to $100,000. But the story did not end there. A year and a half later the leadership team of the organization secured a gift worth several hundreds of thousands of dollars to endow a curatorial position they had created. What a superb return on investment. And it all started with a small concept: choosing to value living within one's means. What a powerful lesson for all—individual, family, or organization.

## Enhancing the Culture of Giving in Your Community

Any time you give your time, your energy, or your money, the culture of giving in your community is enhanced by your commitment. Both Anna and Stella provide outstanding examples of this phenomenon. In Anna's case her gift was time and energy, and in Stella's situation she began with gifts of time and energy, and then expanded to a gift of money, which was structured for an exceptional return on investment. The needs in your community are as diverse as we are individually unique, so feel free to be creative as you develop opportunities.

One obstacle I have encountered with clients regarding the fulfillment of charitable aspirations is a lack of familiarity with, or understanding of, tools that can help them achieve their charitable goals. Therefore, to help you select the tools most likely to enable you to build a culture of giving within your family or community, let us take a moment to review some basic charitable giving tools. Note that some options permit you to gift after your passing and some are structured for gifts made while you are still living:

- A **bequest** is a provision in your will or trust fund, directing funds to a charitable endeavor.

- A **charitable gift annuity** provides income to you (and your spouse or your designated beneficiary) for life in return for a lump-sum charitable gift.

- A **charitable remainder trust** provides a fixed amount of income to you (and your spouse or your designated beneficiary) annually for a specific period of years. Remaining assets (the remainder) are gifted to a charity.

- A **charitable lead trust** provides a fixed amount of income to a charitable endeavor for a specific period of time. Remaining assets return to the donor.

- A **pooled income fund** is a pool of gifts from a number of donors. Donors share in the income generated annually from the pooled funds. At the passing of each donor, his/her proportionate share of principal is gifted to the charity.

- A **retained life estate** transfers ownership of your residence to a charity. You retain the right to live in your gifted property. At your passing the charity may sell the property and make use of the proceeds.

- A **charitable bargain sale** permits you to sell your property to a charity for less than the fair market value. The charity may then sell the property for full value and use the difference to advance its mission.

- A **community foundation** is an organization designed to pool donations into a coordinated investment and grant-making facility. Community foundations are often dedicated to the social improvement of a given place.

- A **private foundation** typically makes grants (donations) to other charities or 501(c)(3) non-profit organizations. A private foundation is defined under section 501(c)(3) of the Internal Revenue code just like any other charitable organization. As with other charitable endeavors, a private foundation must benefit the public in order to maintain its tax-exempt status. For example, in our story about Stella, a private foundation (a charity) gave the $50,000 to the small arts organization (a 501(c)(3) non-profit organization).

- A **donor-advised fund** permits you to set up one account called a donor-advised fund from which you make grants of differing amounts to charities of your choice. It allows an individual to streamline the management of her charitable gifts.

As you can see, there is a wide array of options for cultivating your charitable interests and satisfying your intent to give back. And this list barely scratches the surface of options you might consider. For a comprehensive look at the world of giving, I encourage you to read Laura Arrillaga-Andreessen's *Giving 2.0: Transform Your Giving and Our World*.

## Impact Investing

Before taking an in-depth look at the donor-advised fund—a specific charitable tool that families often find particularly satisfactory—it would be remiss not to introduce impact investing. While impact investing is not technically philanthropic, for investors interested in aligning their money with their values, such investing can serve an important role. Quite simply, impact investments are investments made into companies, organizations, and mutual funds with the intention to generate social and environmental impact alongside a financial return. Another way to think of impact investing is, "Doing well (financially) by doing good."

The four core characteristics of impact investing are:

1. Intention—an investor's intention to have a positive social or environmental impact through investments

2. Investment with return expectations—an investor's expectation to generate a financial return on capital, or at minimum, a return of capital

3. Asset classes—an investor's selection of asset classes designed to target market returns based upon the assumption of risk

4. Impact measurement—an investor's commitment to measure and report upon the social and environmental performance and progress of underlying investments

You may wonder why more investors are not aligning their values with their money by selecting to implement impact investing. Several reasons for this come to mind. First, few financial advisors explore impact investing with their clients unless the client initiates an inquiry requiring them to respond. This paradigm leaves many investors uninformed about options available to them.

Second, one reason impact investing is not explored is because in the past there was widespread concern about the underperformance of what was then called "socially responsible" (now impact) investing. While such concerns no longer need be a deterrent to investors due to the breadth of impact investment choices currently available, that former underperformance concern still lurks in the background.

A third reason impact investing is not broadly embraced is the difficulty investors expect to encounter as they aim to design a risk-appropriate asset allocation. They are uncertain what asset class selections exist with which to build their portfolios. Asset allocation, you may recall, was illustrated in Chapter 4 using the red gravy metaphor. Fortunately, as number three above reveals, there are now a sufficient variety of impact investment asset classes to fulfill investors' desired asset allocation requirements.

Although impact investing is a portfolio-building tool and not a charitable endeavor, it provides another opportunity for investors to fulfill their values. Investors may do well financially while doing good.

## The Donor-Advised Fund

Now let us return to our discussion of dedicated philanthropic tools by examining the features of a donor-advised fund (DAF). The DAF is flexible in a number of ways and, as such, is a useful tool for families:

- It is a single account from which donations may be made to a wide array of charitable causes.
- A relatively small amount of money is needed to establish a DAF account. For example, a community foundation may offer to establish a donor-advised fund for you with a minimum investment of $10,000. A mutual fund company offering such funds usually requires a minimum account investment of $25,000.
- Little administration or reporting is required. The funds invested in your DAF may entitle you to an income tax deduction in the year in which you establish the account. Therefore it is necessary to consult with your accountant about income tax filing procedures.

By the same token, a donor-advised fund can offer families a meaningful learning experience. Let me tell you about Jill, a grandmother with a strong commitment to teach future generations about sharing. As a younger woman Jill had worked hard and had become affluent. As time passed, giving back became a tangible way to express gratitude for the well-being she and her family had achieved. In her middle years, like Stella, she saw the value and importance of serving of boards. Along with board service, she gave financial gifts from time to time without having a specific plan in mind.

Then, one day, she had the good fortune of meeting Gerry Lenfest, the philanthropist, at a Temple University Trustees Dinner, and aspects of her life began to change. As Jill tells her story, after a brief moment of intimidation at being introduced to the rich man seated next to her, she vowed to herself to find a moment during dinner when she could inquire about his foundation. She wanted to know how he had structured the charity to encourage his children to take ownership of grant-making decisions.

As the main course was served, she turned to him and asked how he and his wife had chosen to involve their children in the grant-making decisions of the Lenfest Foundation. He seemed quite comfortable pursuing this line of conversation and told Jill that he did not believe in family foundations. Instead, he believes each individual should own his or her own foundation without interference. He added that he does not believe in perpetuity; therefore his foundation will end no later than thirty years after the death of his wife and himself. And as we learned with our previous description of private foundations, the Lenfests do not give to individuals, only to 501(c)(3) charities.

Jill reported to me that she was inspired to translate the Lenfest family philosophy of owning a charitable account without interference to her own charitable planning. Rather than utilizing a foundation for each family member, however, which would require a larger investment of money than she could commit as well as significant ongoing maintenance, she established a donor-advised fund for each of her children and grandchildren. What a perfect solution, she thought, for helping to introduce her grandchildren to the concept of sharing money as well as the concept of making grants to cause(s) of greatest interest to them.

## Charitable Plan Roadmap

Clearly, Jill's financial aspirations reached far beyond astute investment planning. What a perfect example of the holistic wealth management process in action. Not only was she committed to designing a roadmap for her charitable intentions, she was planning to use sharing with others as a teaching tool for the next generation. Jill decided she wanted a roadmap to illustrate her charitable plan. Perhaps her illustration in Figure 14 will prompt your thinking as you consider the plans you might make.

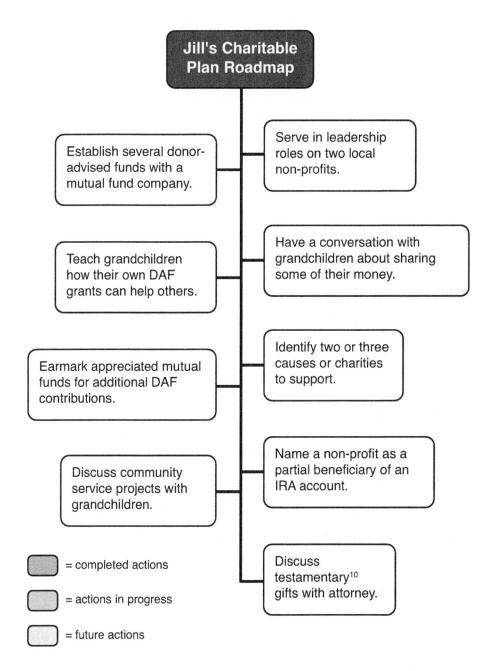

**Figure 14:** Charitable Plan Roadmap

---

[10]Testamentary gifts transfer by will after death.

As you can see, there are a number of steps involved in fulfilling charitable inclinations. Jill's conversation with Gerry Lenfest motivated her to formalize a plan, which she ultimately found satisfying because it led her to have intergenerational conversations about giving. She felt good about enhancing the culture of giving within her family, especially because from these family beginnings, the culture of giving would expand across a larger community.

## Balancing Act Implications

You now have concrete tools to assist you in following your dreams of being a philanthropist. You may wish to give of your time and energy, or your money. You may want to make giving back a family affair. You might prefer to give now or to leave a legacy through your estate plan. Regardless of the choice(s) you make, your gifts enhance a culture of giving with exponential ripple effects of benefit.

One of these benefits is how good you will likely feel. Taking action with respect to philanthropy can affirm your sense of gratitude; it can reinforce the alignment of your values and your money; and finally, your charitable endeavors will likely prove to be a true confidence booster. If your financial advisor has not opened a dialogue with you about planning to fulfill your charitable aspirations, I encourage you to start the conversation. As you remember from our discussion about holistic wealth management in Chapter 5, addressing your financial concerns that go beyond your investment planning, such as charitable planning, may be essential to ensure you achieve all that is important to you.

Should you need just one more push of inspiration, pay a visit to **www.womenmovingmillions.com**. This organization is committed to philanthropy, and it is committed to women, globally. Women Moving Millions is comfortable acknowledging the power of philanthropy and the boldness women can bring to fulfilling their aspirations to give back.

Many women have charitable inclinations but may not have utilized a framework for identifying them or formulated a plan to fulfill them.

The exercises that follow are intended to help you do both: the questionnaire in *Exercise #1* will help you focus on how you prefer to help, and *Exercise #2* offers you a diagram so you can map out or create a picture of your intentions.

### Exercise #1: How I Want to Give Back

Remember that your desire to give back is uniquely yours. To assess whether your charitable aspirations are focused or not, answer the following questions as honestly as you can:

- What am I passionate about?
- If I could make a difference, what arena matters most to me? What comes second?
- If I could spare two hours each week, what cause or organization would I like to help or support in those two hours?
- If I am not already providing assistance, what is holding me back?
- Do I respond to helping in person? Or is long-distance helping just fine for me?
- How much money am I able to contribute to a cause or to an organization?
- Am I interested in making a leadership gift at some point? Generally speaking, a leadership gift is intended to be a major gift to support a particular endeavor and is given in part to motivate other contributors to fill a financial gap with their contributions so the endeavor can proceed. Stella's stability fund contribution is an example of a leadership gift.

### Exercise #2: My Charitable Plan

Jill's charitable planning was illustrated using a mapping diagram (Figure 14). The following sample roadmap (Figure 15) utilizes a number of charitable tools. Compare the sample plan to Jill's Charitable Plan Roadmap.

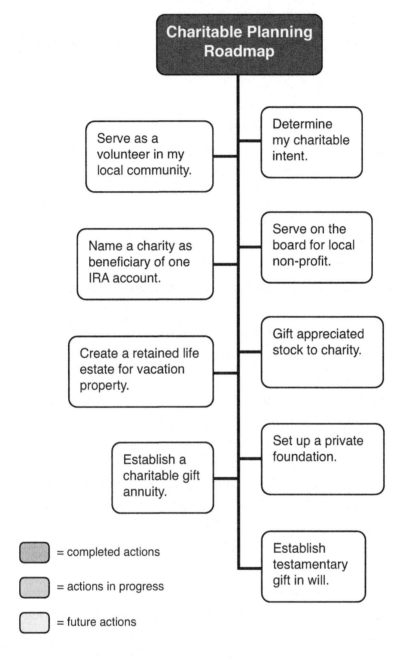

**Figure 15:** Sample Charitable Planning Roadmap

Next, review your answers from *Exercise #1*. You are ready to start formulating your own charitable plan! Visit **Balancingactbook.com**, click on the **Resources** tab, and download the Chapter 8 *Charitable Planning Roadmap* to diagram your intentions.

The door is always open for you to fulfill your charitable aspirations. The women who permitted their stories to be told in Chapter 8 certainly believed this. There is another fundamental door I believe the world needs each of us women to open: the door to serving in leadership roles.

# CHAPTER 9

# Pursue Your Leadership Potential

*"If you think you're too small to make an impact,
try going to bed with a mosquito."*

—Anita Roddick

The preceding chapters have challenged you to manage your wealth, protect your lifestyle, and leave fear behind. They have done so in the context of an emotionally charged subject, money. This chapter contains a pep talk designed to motivate you to meet these challenges by taking actions you may feel insecure about pursuing. The pep talk is founded on my faith in your innate leadership potential. I believe you possess leadership potential you have not fully acknowledged; it is your innate leadership abilities that, when consciously cultivated, empower you to move beyond insecurity.

Why mention actions, money, and leadership in the same breath? In order to manage your wealth effectively, it is necessary to act. And as you take action with respect to your wealth, you guide, shape, or control; in other words, you lead. I have discovered that leading the way or sharing leadership with a spouse regarding one's financial life is a way of cultivating leadership skills.

Even today, leading the way regarding their financial lives represents a sea change for many women. If they choose to share in the leadership of the family finances, this choice presents a new experience. Despite abundant professional accomplishments, the majority of women still delegate the family finances to the leadership purview of husband, and single women often feel compelled to defer to a male relative rather than relying on their own decisions. This chapter will illustrate, with the support of research, that not only are women capable of shared leadership in their professional endeavors, but outcomes improve when men and women work together. Shared leadership in the home regarding the family finances is also likely to deliver better outcomes.

If you find yourself dismissing the idea that you too can lead, consider the following historical perspective. Over the centuries, women leaders generally worked behind the scenes, rarely receiving credit or being recognized for their contributions and impact. Take the example of Ada Lovelace, an English mathematician who was born in 1815. Her unique contribution was the algorithm she developed for a computer that did not yet exist, an accomplishment now thought to qualify her as one of the world's earliest computer-science pioneers. I suspect few of us, when thinking about our computer, would guess we have a woman to thank for its origin.

Our discussion of women and leadership begins with a brief look at American history to offer perspective on the traditional absence of women from formal leadership roles. We will then take a look at the stories of four women who fulfilled their leadership abilities by:

- Raising a child
- Serving as senior executives in corporate America
- Starting a highly successful company as an entrepreneur

As you read this chapter, I encourage you to take notes about your past and present experiences of taking action to meet challenges you encountered in guiding, shaping, and controlling your personal finances. Although your leadership gifts, financial or not, may have been *un*consciously utilized in the past, I believe careful identification of your gifts may secure your commitment to advance your leadership capacity, beginning today.

A brief snapshot of history sheds light on why American women spent decades as second-class citizens rather than consciously cultivating their abilities to contribute as leaders.

## Snapshot of History: Women in America

We are America, the nation who broke away from the British because it was an inalienable right to be free. The United States of America remains the leader of the free world. Critical to our definition of freedom is the right to choose who represents us in government, the right to choose our leaders. But for 144 years after declaring independence in 1776, half of the American population—all of its women—were denied this freedom, this right to choose.

Women were dubbed unable to make decisions as important as choosing for whom to vote. Our fathers and brothers would decide for us. Therefore we did not attain full rights as American citizens until the relentlessly courageous suffragists won us the right to vote in 1920, fewer than one hundred years ago.

A subsequent major milestone for women occurred during World War II. We were permitted, even encouraged, to work outside the home in order to help the war effort. But for the most part women went right back to their home fires following the war. The Civil Rights Movement of the 1960s also resulted in a great leap forward regarding full rights of citizenship for women. The Civil Rights Movement gave voice to the concept of equal opportunity and American women as part of the minority had been deprived of all manner of opportunities.

Equal opportunity meant an expansion of choices. Over the decades of the 1970s and 1980s, we became emancipated from running the family household as our primary life's work. College attendance began to shift away from being a choice predominantly for men. For example, quotas for the number of women allowed to be admitted into a school, such as the three-woman quota for medical school classes enforced by major universities, finally began to give way to the open enrollment model we know today.

The open enrollment model has led to a radical change. Now more women than men pursue and attain college degrees. Well over half of us are engaged in professional careers. American women control $11.2 trillion dollars of wealth. In other words, 39 percent of our nation's investable assets are under the control of women.[11] Currently, women are responsible for making decisions about wealth, not just influencing decisions about wealth from behind the scenes as they did in the past.

In 2020 we will be celebrating the one-hundredth anniversary of the victory of the suffragists, who won us the freedom to vote. They laid the foundation for our slow but steady attainment of the full rights of citizenship. But the battle is far from over. Even today, most women have grown up expecting a man in our lives to make the really important decisions. For example, we have been, and for the most part continue to be, raised in a culture touting men as more financially astute than women. We fear that if we ask questions or try to collaborate regarding the family finances when our husband is in charge, we will be perceived as challenging his abilities, undermining his skills, or worst of all not trusting his judgment.

To embrace our full rights of citizenship, we must give ourselves permission to think of ourselves in a new way. For decades our educational, social, and legal institutions taught us we did not have the aptitude to elect leaders (vote!), to calculate our finances, or to assume leadership roles. It is time to let go of that paradigm forever.

---

[11]"Harnessing the Power of the Purse: Female Investors and Global Growth." Center for Talent Innovation. http://www.talentinnovation.org/publication.cfm?publication=1440

Current research supports the timeliness of embracing our full capacity as leaders. For instance, a growing body of research about women concludes that women have natural strengths that make them powerful agents for leadership effectiveness. Women have also been found to be more powerful catalysts for social change than previously recognized. Lo and behold, analysis is proving we do have what it takes to choose leaders, shape our finances, and assume positions of leadership.

## Leadership Power

Perhaps the findings of this current research are as surprising to you as they were unexpected to experienced researchers John Zenger and Joseph Folkman. These men have analyzed exceptional leadership characteristics for decades. Their diagnostic tools are widely used and respected, and their endeavors are driven by statistics, not an agenda.

The results of their work enabled them to identify traits successful leaders possess. They discovered five primary leadership traits: integrity, initiative, self-development, problem-solving, and a drive for results. Zenger and Folkman have made their names designing powerful tools to test for these qualities as well as to develop them in high-potential executives. That has given them the data to analyze where the qualities are most likely to be found. They have applied their methodology to discover the differences in effectiveness between men and women leaders, too, with the striking result that women outscored men in leadership effectiveness.

Dr. Zenger's analysis of the striking results led to a number of observations he shared with CBS Interactive. They included his perception that women use a more collaborative leadership style as opposed to the typically male command-and-control style. He reported other specifics:

> Women are better listeners, better at building relationships and more collaborative and that makes them better adapted to the demands of modern leadership. For that reason, there is no good reason not to promote women.

He continued with his observations when asked to explain why women have not fared better in the corporate hierarchy.

> I'm somewhat at a loss. Thirty-six percent of men say they want to be CEO, where only 18 percent of women say they do. Women have two jobs—the notorious second shift at home—while men, well, don't do quite so much. And I also think that boards simply lack confidence in women. Few have ever seen a female CEO and don't recognize that women perform better. His message to corporate boards around the world is: Don't worry. Not only can women cope; they'll do better.[12]

As mentioned previously, women have demonstrated their leadership qualities for centuries but most often from behind the scenes. When I first encountered Zenger's five leadership traits—integrity, initiative, self-development, problem-solving, and a drive for results—I was immediately reminded how my client Gwynne applied those traits at home as components of her child-rearing practices.

The story that Gwynne told happened years ago, when her youngest child, a daughter, was not quite three years old. She began her story with a description of her daughter as "obstinate beyond description," and says that today she is still full of energy, ideas, and determination.

Gwynne told her story like this:

> When our daughter was not yet three years old she started to argue and resist nightly when it was time for bed. This continued despite our calm reinforcement of consistent bedtime routines. We would tuck her in. We would take turns reading her the story of her choice. And then the lights were turned off.

---

[12]2013 CBS Interactive, Inc., All Rights Reserved, "Yes, Women Make Better Leaders," Margaret Heffernan, March 26, 2013. http://www.cbsnews.com/news/yes-women-make-better-leaders

The minute we crossed the threshold as we left her room, the wailing would begin. We followed the time-tested parental practice of ignoring her wailing and assumed she would soon drop off to sleep. This strategy had worked just fine with her older brother so it ought to work with her, but it didn't. Her determination remained undiminished.

For the next several nights she got out of bed shortly after lights out with the intention of coming downstairs to join her father and me on the patio. Of course we calmly returned her to bed and reminded her it was now lights out and time to be asleep. Out of frustration, one evening we decided to lock the patio door—hoping that when she realized she couldn't join us she might be deterred. Though she was not thwarted by our actions, the incident resulted in crystallizing the challenge.

Shortly after lights out, our daughter got out of bed again and came downstairs. She headed straight for the (now locked) French doors to the patio of our home. She could easily see through the glass and where we were sitting on the patio. When she realized the door was locked, she started banging on the glass and yelling for us to open the door.

Her banging on the glass caused it to crack within seconds. Terrified by what would happen next as she continued to pound, we raced to the door and opened it.

This family crisis prompted a response that Gwynne now refers to as life-changing. She and her husband admitted to one another they had a problem that needed to be solved. Because they were at a loss about how to communicate effectively with their daughter, they sought professional help.

Although Zenger and Folkman identified the primary traits of effective leaders in corporate and institutional settings, those traits are applicable to family setting as well. Gwynne and her husband displayed integrity when they admitted they had a problem. They showed initiative when they sought professional help, someone who could help parents and child find solutions to their mutual problem. They thus learned ways to communicate with their toddler. In the process of learning new skills based on their daughter's needs, they were soon able to manage their daughter effectively.

You, too, have probably exerted leadership skills in response to your own parenting challenges. And those same skills may have helped you succeed professionally. Your story may be similar to Mandy's, who started working at an entry-level position in the corporate world upon graduating from college. She later married and started a family. Meanwhile she worked her way steadily up the management ladder, always dedicating herself to the assigned tasks and responsibilities and consistently holding herself and her results, to the highest standard. Finally, she became a direct report of the CEO of her company. In other words, she was now one rung of the management ladder below the top position in her firm. The CEO was directly responsible for supervising her work.

She was faced with a dilemma when the CEO made the decision to do a massive company-wide reorganization. She was offered a new role that, in essence, would give her responsibility for half the company. Mandy was excited. As her CEO described the position she was thinking, "Wow. This is a big promotion. I wonder what my new compensation package will be." Because the CEO did not mention compensation, she asked and was told that for now the company was not considering an increase in her compensation because she was already well-paid.

His response surprised and angered Mandy. To accept this new role required more hours on the job. This meant giving up time she would otherwise spend with her young family. On the other hand, she believed she could make a significant contribution in this new role and knew she would embrace the challenges it presented.

Mandy could see she had a problem: a desirable promotion without increased compensation. It was time for some soul-searching. She took the time to have an honest conversation with herself. This led her to acknowledge that while she was accustomed to doing well professionally, her self-image was based upon the values of a novice. For one thing, she had failed to recognize that over the years she had developed the skills to be a valuable senior executive. With this offer on the table it was time to embrace the fact that she was ready, that she had what it took to superbly fulfill the demands of the promotion. Furthermore, had this promotion been offered to a man in the firm, an increase in compensation would have been automatic.

These revelations energized Mandy, and she decided to solve the problem by taking a risk. Before barging ahead, however, she confidentially checked in with a number of men and women in her network. She wanted their perspective regarding her soul-searching revelations and their reactions to the risks involved in raising the promotion without compensation matter with her boss.

Having talked to members of her support network, she now felt prepared for her subsequent conversation with the CEO. She confidently indicated to him that she believed she could without reservation fulfill the duties of the new role and make change in a positive direction for the company. Furthermore, she welcomed the professional challenges it would bring. But this more difficult role would require more of her than her current position. For that additional expenditure of energy, she told him she would also need additional compensation.

This time his response was different. "This is not what I was considering, but I will think about it, and let's revisit this conversation next week." Ultimately, the CEO decided to go to the board and request additional compensation and benefits for Mandy, if she were willing to take on the new role.

Mandy attributed her success in this negotiation largely to the revelations resulting from her soul-searching, which led to a newfound level of confidence. Specifically, the soul-searching endeavors shed light on the value of her contribution to the firm. Armed with this recognition, two things changed for Mandy. First, she was confident asking for a salary increase in light of the increased responsibilities of the new position. And second, she determined she was comfortable walking away from the offer, if necessary.

## A Commitment to Build Diverse Leadership Skills

Mandy demonstrated competence in defining her job-related challenges and seeking support from her professional network in much the same way parents often have to problem-solve in response to the needs of their children. Mandy's professional network was instrumental in supporting her choice to take a risk and ask for competitive compensation in return for the increased value she was being asked to contribute.

Fortunately, today there are a few companies with an established commitment to build leadership skills and cultivate inclusion among their diverse workforce. One example is a particular global biopharmaceutical company. As I read through the Mission and Commitment statements posted on the website of this company, I felt like I was conducting research for impact investing (discussed in Chapter 8). What I discovered was nothing less than astonishing.

This global biopharmaceutical company walks its talk. They take their commitment to economic, social, and environmental sustainability seriously, and extend this same expectation to their partners and suppliers. They embrace a diverse workforce and an inclusive corporate culture. To support their commitment to inclusion and to cultivate diversity of people, perspective, and experience among their employees, they have established employee resource groups.

Employee resource groups are aimed at fulfilling networking, professional, and personal development needs. They have resource groups for Latinos, Pan-Asians, African Americans, women, differently abled employees, and for employees with non-traditional sexual orientations. Their commitment to cultural diversity and inclusion shines through.

Authentic cultural diversity and inclusion are not yet the mainstream for corporate America, nor for our governmental, educational, or non-profit institutions. Why is this particular global biopharmaceutical company different? What are some factors that might have propelled this company to innovate?

Quite possibly the growing body of research affirming the benefit of diversity and inclusion has impacted this firm's strategy. A succinct synthesis of this research was presented in an article by Sallie L. Krawcheck, Chair of Pax Ellevate Management, LLC, entitled: "The Big Idea 2015: Inclusive Capitalism = A More Prosperous Capitalism." Highlights of the benefits of diversity and inclusion include:

- Innovation increases
- Companies get better results—higher returns on capital, lower risk, greater long-term focus, more substantive client focus
- Companies are pushed toward greater meaning and purpose
- Investors push companies to define their impact on the world around them
- Families benefit

Regardless of the reasons for a commitment to diverse leadership within this particular biopharmaceutical company, their domestic East Coast office has chosen to focus on keeping talented women in the workforce. And this East Coast office has a strong commitment to sponsoring and mentoring women, so they may attain and serve effectively in senior leadership roles. To accomplish these goals, they focus on the need to create change at the feeling level. I interviewed a woman in a senior leadership position, and she described the feeling level change in this way: "We have a singular goal to move women along the spectrum from being given permission to achieve to empowering them to achieve."

Creating such a change is both lofty and fundamental, but often something as basic as lifestyle balance interferes. (See Zenger's comment about women's notorious second shift at home, mentioned earlier in this chapter.) For instance, it is not unusual for women to resist moving up the ranks because they assume it will just be too complicated to manage a very responsible job, complete with traveling, in tandem with fulfilling home responsibilities.

The company's commitment to cultivate women in senior leadership roles shone through in a recent event hosted by senior management (mostly men). A networking event with dinner was aimed specifically at female middle managers. The goal was "getting to know you." Before this event, these women did not know senior management, and senior management did not really know the women in middle management positions.

A striking change from typical networking events, all attendees received the bios of one another, with photos, prior to the event. This enabled attendees to become familiar with each participant ahead of time. They were able to arrive at the event ready to engage in meaningful conversation when they met in person. This set the stage for proactive listening and brought about more effective networking. The tactic of providing pre-event bios reinforced an important goal for the evening: that of listening and having authentic relationship-building experiences during the group's time together.

## Resources for Women

Not all women have the resources of a successful global company available. However, a growing number of resources are available to women, resulting in part from attaining full rights of citizenship as a result of the suffragists' struggle almost one hundred years ago. Gwynne faced a call to action on the home front that required her to assemble resources to support her parenting needs. Mandy faced a call to action regarding a senior-level job offer; she, too, had to assemble resources to respond successfully. Just as the global pharmaceutical company embraced the goal to move women along the spectrum from being given permission to achieve to empowering them to achieve, so does the work of Wall

Street's Sallie Krawcheck seek to advance women. One of her endeavors was to establish a mutual fund, Pax Ellevate Global Women's Index Fund, with an objective of investing only in companies with at least 30 percent diversity on their boards.

Other women, too, have founded endeavors and initiatives that help pave the way for all of us. Some examples include:

- Equal pay—**http://equalpaynegotiations.com**
- Diverse boards—**http://www.30percentcoalition.org**
- Running for office—**https://voterunlead.org/go-run/ training-events**
- Attaining the executive suite—**http://www.ionwomen.org**
- Focus on social change—**http://drexel.edu/vision2020**

## The Woman Entrepreneur

During these transformational times, women are also turning to their greatest asset, themselves, as they launch into positions of leadership. They are doing this by starting their own businesses at a "torrid" pace, according to an American Express analysis of U. S. Census bureau figures. Between 1997 and 2014, the number of women-owned business in the U.S. rose by 68 percent. Women are starting businesses twice as fast as men because they want to "seize control of their time and schedule at work."[13] Unfortunately, women continue to earn about 25 percent less than men for the same work, and fewer than 2 percent of women-owned firms reach the million-dollar revenue threshold. This statistic has remained unchanged in the last decade despite the rapid pace of women's entrepreneurship.

---

[13]Harvard Business Review, "More Women Starting New Businesses Isn't Necessarily Good News," Morra Aarons-Mele. June 25, 2014. https://hbr.org/2014/06/more-women-starting-businesses-isnt-necessarily-good-news

Although statistics show us general trends, there are always outliers. Entrepreneur and esthetician Danuta Mieloch (rescuespa.net) is one of them. Notably, she was willing to share her story, which may provide inspiration for you as it has for me.

She immigrated to the United States from Poland about twenty-five years ago and spoke no English. Her husband and sister were living in New York City, so that is where her life in America began. Danuta studied English as she rode the train daily to her waitressing job. Along the way she learned the importance of acquiring interpersonal skills, networking skills and of saving money. Even if you are by nature a spender (which she admits she is), you need to adopt the motto, "Spend less than you earn to be ahead of the game."

Following a divorce and relentless saving so she could live for a year without earning a dime, Danuta moved to Philadelphia in 2004. She took the first steps of opening her now thriving business, Rescue Spa, employing such strategic decisions as:

- Renting a larger space than she needed and planning to not use all the space when she first opened her doors
- Deciding to engage in the business by giving facials because that is a strength
- Joining all organizations in the immediate Center City Philadelphia area to promote her services
- Offering more complimentary services than other spas to build appeal
- Adhering to the highest possible standards

Danuta began with five employees, and eleven years later, in 2015, she has fifty employees. I asked her whether she found it easy or difficult to delegate, a common problem for self-starters. She replied that she is good at delegating because she does not know how to do everything.

I then asked how she would describe her leadership qualities. She responded that her most important leadership skill is that she practices what she preaches. She continued, "I am always here. My commitment is a prime example for my staff. And I must personally be the image I am purporting for my clients to achieve. Skincare is a commitment and a process, not a one-shot endeavor."

Danuta's comment about effective skincare—"a commitment and a process, not a one-shot endeavor"—crystallizes holistic wealth management. Holistic wealth management is a lifelong commitment and requires a process. The process is a framework designed to support your life's journey. Inherent in the process are the need for flexibility and the need to adapt and flow with changes in the rhythms of your style of living as they occur.

## Balancing Act Implications

This chapter challenged you to act in order to manage your wealth effectively. It posited the thesis that as you take action regarding your wealth, whether sharing responsibility with your spouse or going solo, you build your confidence and cultivate your leadership skills. Research was presented that concludes women are not only capable of leadership in professional and other endeavors, but that outcomes improve when men and women share leadership roles.

Certainly we have all read reports about the unprecedented amount of wealth baby boomers are poised to inherit. Women who inherit wealth often face a call to action and a call to lead—to guide, shape, and control—just like moms, professionals, and entrepreneurs. In fact, perhaps your call to action and call to lead will be precipitated because you receive an inheritance. If so, the question likely to spring to mind immediately is, "What should I do with all this money?"

Whether that question is on your mind or whether you started reading this book with concerns about your existing wealth planning strategy, your journey has begun in earnest. You have taken the time to enhance your understanding of how to manage your wealth, how to protect your lifestyle now and into retirement, and what to do to leave fear behind. Completing the exercises has augmented your comprehension of wealth management straight talk, particularly as it applies to how women perceive and prefer making decisions about their money.

You have read the stories of many women and discovered the variety of choices they faced as they aimed to achieve the ultimate balancing act, balancing their values, needs, and interests within the context of their whole style of living. You learned, as Danuta eloquently stated, such aims require "a commitment and a process, not a one-shot endeavor." Congratulate yourself on the effort you have made, on your newborn readiness to advance your own story, your own balancing act in fulfillment of your personal values, needs, and interests.

# About the Author

I embarked on my first career as a teacher in a poverty-stricken area of Philadelphia, Pennsylvania, in 1974. My hope and dream was to help each student embrace education as a fundamental life tool. With this multi-faceted tool, I reasoned, the door to opportunity would begin to open for them. Poverty could be left behind.

I quickly learned that my formula for social change was simplistic. No matter how crucial education was, it wasn't enough. My students needed other fundamental tools, tools that went beyond what I could hope to impart in my role as teacher. They needed confidence in their ability to create a different life and the intention to pursue it.

My commitment to creating a better life for myself, better than the one I had experienced in my youth, was tested in my early forties when my husband was diagnosed with cancer. What a wake-up call. My thoughts raced. "If he isn't here anymore, would I need to make any major changes such as pursuing a different career?" It was terrifying to consider his illness and the possible consequences. But my fear became exponentially greater as it dawned on me that it was time for me to move on from public-school teaching.

Fortunately, during that time I did not suffer from financial fear because I had been investing in a supplemental retirement plan for about twenty years prior to my husband's illness. While I had no idea what the future held, I did know I had funds set aside to help me bridge the income gap I was likely to experience while becoming established in a new career.

As I reflected on next steps for me, I realized that money, just like education, is a basic life tool. But as I learned during my teaching career, to experience the full benefits of a basic life tool, one needs confidence in one's ability to use it effectively as well as the intention to do so. My calling became clear: I wanted to become a financial planner to help others make the right choices at pivotal times in their lives without financial concerns, just as I had been able to do.

For most of us, making the right choices is a balancing act. Not only are we faced with balancing our values, needs, and interests, but our choices are complicated by the need to balance all of this within the context of our whole style of living. *Balancing Act: Wealth Management Straight Talk for Women* tells the story of many women. It records the choices they faced, the life balance for which they aimed, and the results they experienced.

Contact me today to start a conversation about your intention to make the right financial choices—within the context of your whole style of living.

**Joslyn G. Ewart, CFP**®
Founding Principal
Entrust Financial LLC®
940 West Valley Road, #1902
Wayne, PA 19087
610-687-3515
info@entrustfinancial.com
www.balancingactbook.com
www.entrustfinancial.com

CPSIA information can be obtained at www.ICGtesting.com
Printed in the USA
BVOW06s1930020916

461009BV00001B/1/P

9 780997 659948